Powers

Hiawatha

AND THE IROQUOIS LEAGUE

Alvin Josephy's Biography Series of American Indians

Hiawatha

AND THE IROQUOIS LEAGUE

Written by Megan McClard · George Ypsilantis

INTRODUCTION BY ALVIN M. JOSEPHY, JR.
ILLUSTRATED BY FRANK RICCIO

Silver Burdett Press

Project editors: Nancy Furstinger (Silver Burdett Press)
Mark Davies & Della Rowland (Kipling Press)
Designed by Mike Hortens

10 9 8 7 6 5 4 3 2   (Lib. ed.)
10 9 8 7 6 5 4 3   (Pbk. ed.)

Library of Congress Cataloging-in-Publication Data

McClard, Megan.
Hiawatha and the Iroquois league / written by Megan McClard &
George Ypsilantis ; introduction by Alvin M. Josephy, Jr., ;
illustrations by Frank Riccio.
    p.   cm. — (Alvin Josephy's biography series of
American Indians)
Bibliography: p. 122
Summary: Follows the life of the Iroquois leader who contributed
to the formation of a league of Indian nations and discusses the
actions and effects of this league as it interacted with the white
colonists up through the eighteenth century.
1. Hiawatha, 15th cent. 2. Iroquois Indians—Biography—Juvenile
literature. 3. Iroquois Indians—Tribal government—Juvenile
literature. 4. Indians of North America—New York (State)—
Biography—Juvenile literature. 5. Indians of North America—New
York (State)—Tribal government—Juvenile literature.
[1. Hiawatha, 15th cent. 2. Iroquois Indians—Biography.
3. Indians of North America—New York (State)—Biography.
4. Iroquois Indians—Tribal government. 5. Indians of North
America—New York (State)—Tribal government.] I. Ypsilantis,
George. II. Riccio, Frank, ill. III. Title. IV. Series.
E99.I7H48b   1989
974.7'01'0924—dc19
[B]
[92]   88-37503
CIP
AC
ISBN 0-382-09568-5 (lib. bdg.)
ISBN 0-382-09757-2 (pbk.)

Contents

To my children,
Michael, Kevin, Elizabeth,
Peter, and Anne.
M.M.

Although this book is based on real events and real people, some dialogue, a few thoughts, and several local descriptions have been reconstructed to make the story more enjoyable. It does not, however, alter the basic truth of the story we are telling.

Unless indicated otherwise, the Indian designs used throughout this book are purely decorative, and do not signify a particular tribe or nation.

∞   ∞   ∞

Introduction

For 500 years, Christopher Columbus has been hailed as the "discoverer" of America. But Columbus only discovered America for his fellow Europeans, who did not know of its existence. America was really discovered more than 10,000 years before the time of Columbus by people who came across the Bering Strait from Siberia into Alaska. From there they spread south to populate both North and South America. By the time of Columbus, in fact, there were millions of descendants of the true discoverers of America living in all parts of the Western Hemisphere. They inhabited the territory from the northern shores of Alaska and Canada to the southern tip of South America. In what is now the United States, hundreds of tribes, large and small, covered the land from Maine and

Map of
Continental United States
American Indians

Florida to Puget Sound and California. Each tribe had a long and proud history of its own. America was hardly an "unknown world," an "unexplored wilderness"—except to the Europeans who gazed for the first time upon its forests and rivers, its prairies and mountains.

From the very beginning, the newcomers from Europe had many mistaken notions about the people whose ancestors had been living in America for centuries. At first Columbus thought he had reached the East Indies of Asia, and he called the people Indians. The name took hold and remains to this day. But there were more serious misconceptions that had a tragic effect on relations between the Indians and the Europeans. These misconceptions led to one of the greatest holocausts in world history. Indians were robbed of their possessions, their lands, and the lives of countless numbers of their people.

Most Europeans never really understood the thinking, beliefs, values, or religions of the Indians. The Indian way of life was so different from that of the Europeans, who had inherited thousands of years of diverse backgrounds, religions, and ways of thinking and acting. The Europeans looked down on the Indians as strange and different, and therefore inferior. They were ignorant in the way they treated the Indians. To the white people, the Indians were "savages" and "barbarians," who either had to change their ways and become completely like the Europeans or be destroyed.

At the same time, many Europeans came as conquerors. They wanted the Indians' lands and the resources of those lands—resources such as gold, silver, and furs. Their greed, their superior weapons, and their contempt for the Indians' "inferior" ways led to many wars. Of course the Indians fought back to protect the lives of their people, their lands, their religions, their freedoms, their very way of life. But the

Europeans—and then their American descendants—assumed that the Indians were all fierce warriors who fought simply because they loved to fight. Only in recent years have we come to see the Indians as they really are—people who would fight when their lives and freedom were at stake. People who were fun-loving children, young lovers, mothers who cried for the safety and health of their families, fathers who did their best to provide food, wise old people who gave advice, religious leaders, philosophers, statesmen, artists, musicians, storytellers, makers of crafts. Yes, and scientists, engineers, and builders of cities as well. The Indian civilizations in Mexico and Peru were among the most advanced the world has ever known.

This book gets beneath the surface of the old, worn-out fables to tell a real story of the Indians—to help us understand how the Indians looked at the world. When we understand this, we can see not only what they did, but why they did it. Everything here is accurate history, and it is an exciting story. And it is told in such a way that we, the readers, can imagine ourselves back among the Indians of the past, identifying ourselves with their ways of life, beliefs, and destinies. Perhaps in the end we will be able to ask: What choices would we have had? How would we ourselves have responded and behaved?

Hiawatha is one of America's most famous and, at the same time, least-known Indians. For many years, readers all over the world have known about Henry Wadsworth Longfellow's poem *Hiawatha*. But Longfellow's work was mostly fiction, filled with the white people's romantic ideal of what Indian culture and beliefs were like. Longfellow even mixed up the Indian nation and homeland of his hero. Hiawatha was actually a member of the Iroquois tribe, living in what is now New York State. Longfellow said he was an Ojibwa, or Chippewa, Indian from the Great Lakes of the Midwest. Today that would be the same thing as writing a poem about an Englishman who lived in London—but making him an Italian who lived in Rome!

The true story of Hiawatha is much more interesting than the poem. It illustrates how the Indians were able to govern themselves under political systems far more advanced and sophisticated than most white people imagined them to be. This is the story of what might be called an early Indian version of the United Nations. It was the famous Iroquois League, which existed many years before the American Revolution. Many perceptive white people thought it was more democratic and representative of its people than any government then existing in Europe. In fact, there are those who believe the league made a deep impression on Benjamin Franklin and other founders of America's constitutional form of government.

—Alvin M. Josephy, Jr.

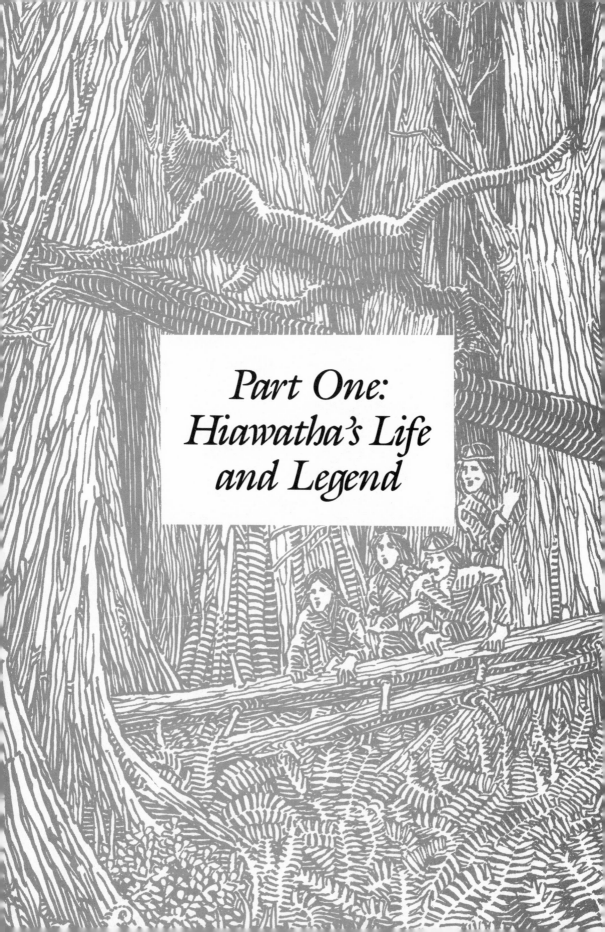

Part One: Hiawatha's Life and Legend

Iroquois Childhood

The longhouse was quiet. Inside nearly everyone was asleep, lying head to toe along the two sleeping benches that stretched the length of the walls. Every so often a log smoldering on one of the hearths would pop, sending a spark into the smoky room, or someone would snore or call out in his or her sleep. A young woman sat up, wrapped herself in a fur robe, and slipped past her sisters and out the door. She walked quickly through the gate of the spiked wooden fence, called a *palisade*, that encircled the village. Outside the village, the Onondaga woman paused for a moment, then hurried toward the woods beside the creek. There, in the light of the full moon, she gave birth to a baby boy she named Hiawatha. She inspected him, washed him in icy creek water, and wrapped him in furs. Then she returned to the longhouse, where her mother and sisters met her.

Hiawatha's grandmother unwrapped him, examined the umbilical cord, counted his fingers and toes, and touched his black hair with her calloused hand. While one of his aunts brought the new mother a ladle of cool water, another arranged the furs on the sleeping bench for her.

The next morning, his grandmother made thick, unleavened corncakes on the hearth while Hiawatha's aunt diapered him with dry moss, wrapped him in rabbit skins, and gave him to his mother to nurse. A small cousin, curious about this new creature, poked a finger at him and was quickly whisked away and given a cornhusk doll to play with.

Hiawatha's mother said, "He's so tiny. All night I listened for his breathing."

His grandmother said, "He'll be off hunting before you blink two times. Enjoy him while he is with you."

"I wish his father could see him," the mother said. She knew that her husband and the rest of the men from the village would not return from the hunt for another moon, when the time came for the midwinter celebration.

Hiawatha's people, the Onondagas, were one of the Iroquois nations. His life would have been much the same had he been born a member of another Iroquois tribe, such as Cayuga, Oneida, Seneca, or Mohawk. All the Iroquois lived the same way and spoke dialects of the same language.

This was the quietest time of year in the village. The harvest was over. From one end of the longhouses to the other, colorful ears of corn were hung on every pole and along the walls. The weather was still warm enough in the daytime to leave the doors at each end of the longhouses open. At night it became quite cold again, and the doors were covered with bearskins.

The families of Hiawatha's mother—her grandmother, two great aunts, three aunts, and sisters—all lived in one longhouse. Each family kept its own hearth fire. There was little privacy, but sometimes a woman hung hides to screen her area from the families who lived beside her. Hiawatha's mother had hung a bearskin beside his sleeping place, to protect him from the drafts that blew through the roof holes and from the smoke that curled up from the fire. There were no windows in the longhouse, only the roof holes that served as both chimney and skylight.

Hiawatha's great-grandmother owned the longhouse. The other longhouses in the village also belonged to older women, or *matrons*, whose married daughters and granddaughters each ruled a separate hearth in the dwelling. One longhouse might have ten hearths, another only five. One of Hiawatha's great aunts, whose husband was a leader, called a *sachem*, lived with her family in a single bark house just outside the village gate. Hiawatha's mother thought her aunt must be very lonely.

In the spring Hiawatha's mother carried him in a cradleboard on her back, as she planted corn in the village cornfield with her aunts, sisters, and cousins. Hiawatha cried very little, soothed by the rhythmic motion of his mother's body as she broke the earth with her stone hoe.

When Hiawatha was older he enjoyed watching his mother dig small holes with her wooden shovel and carefully place two or three kernels of corn in each one. Planting was like a game. She hid the kernels from the crows and squirrels by patting a little hill of dirt over them. Later a little corn plant would appear. After that, she would plant beans or squash seed beside the corn, and soon leaves would pop up where the seeds had been.

Hiawatha's father and uncles were not allowed in the field. The Onondagas, like other Iroquois people, thought it would anger their gods if men meddled in agriculture. They didn't touch the corn until it was ready to be eaten. The only thing men could grow was the tobacco they used in their rituals. Men had other responsibilities, equally important. They hunted, fished, made weapons, and waged war.

Like the other Onondaga children, Hiawatha stayed with his mother wherever she went until he was five or six years old. She never spanked him and rarely scolded him. If he made a mistake, his mother and his aunts would tease him in front of his cousins. Once he asked his grandmother to tell him a story.

"I can't do that," she said.

"Yes you can. You know lots of stories," Hiawatha insisted.

"I know many stories," she said, "but I can't tell them until after the harvest."

"Why not?" Hiawatha asked.

"Winter is the time for stories," his grandmother said.

Then she turned to his aunt and his cousins, who were nearby. "Hiawatha would have a bee sting my tongue," she said to them. "Or he would let the birds forget to fly away from the Great Bear. Explain to him why I can't tell him stories until the snow comes."

One of his female cousins said, "Who doesn't know that! Grandmother tells such good stories that the vines on the outside of the longhouse might listen and forget to grow squash. Or a bear might forget to crawl into her cave. Or . . ." After a few minutes of this, Hiawatha began to feel foolish, and had learned a valuable lesson.

Occasionally, the adults had to discipline the children. One form of discipline always worked—the False Faces. Hiawatha and his cousins sometimes annoyed the grownups by jumping up and down on the sleeping bench or teasing a younger child to tears or greedily eating more than their share at the Wild Strawberry Festival. At such times one of the adults would say, "Have it your way. The False Faces will get you, and then you'll wish you had listened to us."

The False Faces were members of a society who wore carved, wooden masks that represented *Flying Heads*, forest-dwelling evil spirits, and other bad creatures from the spirit world. Hiawatha's grandfather had told him how the evil spirits had come into being. The old man repeated the story of the first woman, who fell from the sky and gave birth to two sons. One son was the creator of everything good. The other was the creator of the Flying Heads and other demons that lived in the woods, and even in the souls of human beings.

Sometimes Hiawatha had trouble going to sleep at night. He saw faces everywhere in the flickering shadows of the longhouse, and even more frightening ones when he closed his eyes!

Sometimes the way Onondaga children were reared was harsh, but there was a good reason. Hiawatha's mother told him that an Onondaga man had to be as strong as the trees in the forest. So, in the winter, when the wind sang in the trees and the smoke from the hearths hung over the village, she took him to the stream that flowed past the sweat lodge. She dunked him in the water that was so cold a thin film of ice had formed at its edges—so cold that he couldn't breathe.

In spring, when Hiawatha was about six, everything changed. He was no longer a baby. Instead he went with the other boys to roam in the woods. They would stay in the forest for days at a time, without shelter, finding their own food. He learned to find berries and potatolike tubers and to snare wild game. Although his mother was still responsible for disciplining him, he no longer spent his days in the cornfield with women, nor did he play with girls and nursing babies. He was not meant to grow corn; he was meant to be a warrior, a medicine man, or even a sachem.

That spring he began to learn the men's work. One day he watched one of his uncles girdle the trees that would be burned the next year to enlarge the cornfield. With his light stone ax, called a *tomahawk*, the uncle cut a belt of bark from the tree.

"Why do you do that to the tree?" Hiawatha asked.

"To kill it," his uncle replied.

Hiawatha said, "Did you ever kill a man with your ax?"

His uncle said, "Of course not. The ax is a very good tool, but a very bad weapon."

Hiawatha said, "Why do you kill people anyway?"

His uncle said, "It's just the way life is. If someone does wrong to you, you have to get even." Then he said, "Why don't you go find your cousins. You aren't supposed to play in these woods. They're dangerous. See that dead branch?" He pointed to one of the trees the men had girdled the year before. "It's about to fall. You go on now before the False Faces get you."

Hiawatha thought the men did more interesting things than the women, but not on a regular basis. For example, it was the men's job to build the bark houses. They cut the timbers, set them in holes they had dug, and lashed them together. Then they made a roof of saplings and shingled the whole house with overlapping strips of elm bark. For a few days the men would sweat and grunt, but then the house would be finished, and that would be that. They wouldn't build another house until the whole village moved, many moons later.

The women's tasks required daily effort, but the men had little to do, especially in the summer. The women worked in the cornfield or pounded dried corn into flour with a wooden mortar or made moccasins and rope out of cornhusks. The men sat in the shade—the old ones talking about the old days, the young ones playing games.

Hiawatha thought the best thing the men did was play games. He especially liked to watch the young braves play baggataway, the game now called lacrosse. It was intended to help them prepare for war, but Hiawatha didn't dwell on that. He just enjoyed the excitement as the two teams raced back and forth swinging their netted sticks at the deerskin ball, trying to score a goal. When the game was over, everyone shouted and threw things onto the field. Although Hiawatha did not yet understand the game, he shouted along with the rest of them.

In winter Hiawatha's older cousins played snow snake, a game in which they took turns sliding a long, polished hickory stick along an iced trough of snow, to see who could make it travel farthest. First his cousins dragged a log lengthwise through the snow to make a trench that was one foot deep and five hundred yards long. The trench was packed and smoothed until it

was very slick. The sticks were sometimes nine feet long and looked like thin snakes as they shot along the icy trough.

Although the game looked easy, it took great skill and strength. After the young men were finished, Hiawatha and the other small boys tried the game, but they could never get their own sumac sticks to skim the snow as they were supposed to. Soon the boys were hurling the sticks like javelins at rabbits or at each other.

After the harvest, in late fall, the men's work began as they prepared for the yearly hunting expedition. Most of the men left the village and went deep into the woods after game. Hiawatha's father, uncles, and cousins made arrowheads out of flint, a very hard stone. They *fletched*, or fitted feathers on, the arrow shafts so that they drilled through the air, flying straight and true.

As the men made their hunting tools, the women repaired deerskin leggings, moccasins, and robes. Cornmeal cakes and maple sugar were packed for the men to carry with them on the hunt. When the moon was right, the hunting party set off. The men traveled far from home, camping in the woods for many nights. When they returned, they brought enough dried venison for the winter, and there was a great celebration.

One day before the hunt, Hiawatha was running his fingers over his father's bow. Watching him, his father said, "Go ahead. Try it." Hiawatha held the bow before him and pulled the string as hard as he could, but he could not bend the bow. His father said, "Someday you will shoot a great stag, but not today." Then he took the bow from Hiawatha and pulled the string back easily. When he let go, the bowstring hummed. Hiawatha knew that he could join the hunting party only after he had proven himself by killing a deer unassisted.

2
Growing Up

The Iroquois celebrated six major thanks-giving festivals during the year with danc-ing, singing, and speeches. In late winter each of the tribes held the Maple Festival to give thanks for the maple sap they used to sweeten their food. In late spring they celebrated the planting of the corn. Next, in early summer, came a festival for the wild strawberries, which they ate sweetened with maple sugar. The Green Corn Festival took place in late summer, with feasts, prayers, songs, and thanksgiving dances to the earth, water, sun, moon, and stars. In fall, in celebration of the crops of corn, squash, and dried beans that would nourish them throughout the year, the Iroquois held the Harvest Festival.

Hiawatha's favorite festival was the Midwinter, or New Year's, Festival, which went on for days. Each year he noticed something he had never understood before. The festival began with the Big Heads. These men wore buffalo robes and stopped at each longhouse to announce that the New Year had come. As Hiawatha grew older, he recognized his uncles under the robes and called out their names.

After the Big Heads came the members of the False Face Society, a group of medicine men who wore grotesque wooden masks. They went from dwelling to dwelling doing dances to ward off evil spirits that had caused illnesses and to renew past cures.

The dances of the False Faces during Midwinter Festival renewed the power of the healings the medicine men had made in the past. After they danced, the Big Heads went to every longhouse in the village, stirring the embers in each hearth with a paddle. When Hiawatha asked his mother why they stirred up the fire, she said, "Because this is the new year, a time to rekindle life and get rid of the ashes of the past."

Much of the Midwinter Festival was devoted to dreams. Like other Iroquois people, the Onondagas paid very close attention to their dreams. They believed that dreams revealed unconscious needs, or *ondinnonks*. One day, Hiawatha asked his father why dreams were so important. His father said, "Through dreams you will know yourself. Dreams come at night to tell you your ondinnonk."

Hiawatha asked, "What is an ondinnonk?"

"An ondinnonk is an ondinnonk," his father replied. "It's what your soul must have. Your soul often tells what it needs through your dreams. If you don't pay attention to your ondinnonk, your soul becomes sick and makes your body sick."

Once one of Hiawatha's uncles was sick with a very bad fever and dreamed of a bluejay flying out of the woods and stealing corn. Hiawatha's grandmother called the medicine men to his bedside to guess the ondinnonk of the dream. The medicine men guessed the ondinnonk was symbolized by three blue feathers from the tail of a jay. Hiawatha's uncles and cousins set out immediately to snare a bluejay and pluck its tail feathers. Shortly after they returned with the feathers, the sick uncle recovered.

After the festivities the Iroquois gathered in their lodges to talk about their dreams so they could rid themselves of

troubling thoughts. One man was told in a dream that all dreamers should go from hearth to hearth, posing a riddle about their own dreams. Whoever guessed the ondinnonk would then have to give it to the dreamer. Hiawatha's grandmother had dreamed of a beautiful basket woven of cornhusks, just like the one her youngest daughter had made. She went to that daughter's hearth and said, "What can hold the sunlight and the moonlight but not the rain?" The daughter thought for a long time. Finally, she guessed that it was a basket, and gave her mother the basket in her dreams.

As a child, Hiawatha had especially liked the part of the Midwinter Festival when an old woman of the village took the boys from fireside to fireside to beg for presents. If they were given a present, they would sing or dance; if not, they would steal something. But the older he became, the more he liked the last part of the celebration. Members of various societies visited every longhouse to do their special dance. The Buffalo Society butted heads; the False Faces appeared as clowns; the Husk Faces—warriors who wore masks made of cornhusks—dressed as women.

By the time the Midwinter Festival was finished, there had been so much celebration that Hiawatha was almost thankful to return to routine village life. He looked forward to spending time with his friends, hunting small game during the day, and sitting beside the hearth at night.

Then one morning just before dawn, Hiawatha awoke to screams and whoops and braves dashing half-asleep for their clubs. By the time he understood what was going on, it was over. A war party of Cayugas had crept through the village gate and entered one of the bark houses. They had killed two braves, captured their wives, and escaped into the woods. The Cayugas were avenging the deaths of two of their young warriors who had been killed by Onondagas.

3
Warfare

The late-winter Maple Festival was over, and the snows were gone. There were fresh bear tracks on the bank, since the bears' great winter sleep was over. Still the predawn air was brisk and the water cold as the tense, silent band of red-painted Onondagas waded chest-deep in the rushing creek. The creek was deeper now than at any time of year, but the men knew the way across. They did not hesitate. Most of them had come this way many times before. It was the warpath that led to a sleeping Cayuga village. Sixty red-painted braves emerged one by one from the creek. They did not notice the bone-chilling wind that blew through the maple forest. The warriors were intent on their purpose: battle!

Hiawatha's uncles felt nothing. Their minds were hard and determined. Tradition demanded a life for a life. Warfare was a man's very purpose in life. Since creation itself, Onondaga men had been given the duty of killing, whether it was Cayugas, Hurons, bears, or the trees of the forest. The Creator had made women to bring forth life and sustain it; men were made to hunt and fight. Life and death were like the seasons.

Onondaga men were given the duty of killing, whether it was Cayugas, Hurons, bears, or the trees of the forest. The Creator had made women to bring forth life and sustain it; men were made to hunt and fight. Life and death were like the seasons.

The Onondagas were getting revenge for the recent Cayuga raid. For the two Onondagas killed in the last raid, two Cayugas must die. In exchange for the Onondaga women, Cayuga women must be captured. It was a bloody game, and the score was kept in scalps and prisoners.

Each of the raiders was armed with a bow, a quiver of arrows, and a knobbed war club the length of a man's arm. As they came out of the creek, they began to spread out through the forest. They would approach the Cayuga village from all sides to cut off all escape routes.

One of Hiawatha's young cousins heard every bird stir as he crept toward the village. His heart was pounding. This was his chance to prove that he was brave, that he was a man. He knew what could happen to him today. He could return with

Knobbed war club

15

the war party to his village, perhaps with a captive or two. Or he could be captured and tortured by the Cayugas.

His mouth was dry. Just last year he had watched his own people torture a Seneca and a Mohawk. His brother said the torture allowed the victims to show their strength of spirit. The Seneca warrior had screamed out once—a deep, terrible sound. The Mohawk had talked and sung for three days while the Onondagas tormented him with fire. He was very brave and died with honor.

The young Onondaga warrior could see the spiked wooden fence that encircled the village. He could smell the smoke coming from the village houses. Thinking he heard a noise in the woods ahead, he stopped, club poised. Another bird, he thought. Only a few yards farther he saw two Cayuga hunters, lying dead with the game still in their hands. Onondaga scouts had surprised them. These hunters would not return to warn their village. If their souls were worthy, they would go instead to join their ancestors in the Forest Beyond the Red Lakes of the Sunset. The young brave crept past the dead hunters to the edge of the forest, where he waited breathlessly for a signal from the scouts.

Suddenly, he heard an owl screech, the sound he had been waiting for. He ran toward the palisaded wall, climbed it quickly and silently, and bolted for the nearest bark house. While two of his cousins ran through the door, he clambered onto the roof. He had meant to drop through the roof hole, but an ember flew into one of his eyes, and his lungs filled with smoke. He hardly noticed an arrow when it pierced his thigh.

By the time the young brave slid off the roof of the bark house, the whole village was awake; children were screaming; one of the longhouses was in flames; and his own brothers and cousins were vanishing through the gate. He tried to run but fell to the ground and was immediately surrounded by Cayugas.

When the raid was over the Cayugas took him into a bark house, gave him black shanks tea for the pain, and sent for a medicine man. The medicine man removed the arrow from his thigh and covered the wound with a poultice made of herbs. One of the women brought him a bowl of hominy. Hiawatha's cousin knew that the kindness did not mean he would escape torture. Prisoners were usually nursed back to health before being tortured to death.

There was a chance, however, that the Cayugas might adopt him. The women of the village would make that decision. He would be brought before the matrons, and if there was a widow who needed a husband, the young warrior might be given to her. If so he would live out his life as a Cayuga. As it happened, the matrons did decide to spare his life, after looking him over very thoroughly and holding several conferences. They gave him to a young widow whose husband had been killed the year before by Onondagas.

Hiawatha's cousin thought this was not the worst thing that could have happened. His life as a Cayuga would not be much different from his life as an Onondaga. They were both Iroquois tribes who spoke the same language and lived in long-houses that were owned by women. After all, a warrior did not get to choose his marriage partner anyway. And he did not marry someone from his own close-knit clan but went to live in the longhouse of his wife's people. Besides, he may have admired the Mohawk who talked and sang for three days while being roasted, poked, and hacked at, but he certainly had not envied him!

4
Becoming a Man

Like other boys his age, when Hiawatha was about sixteen years old, he was taken into the woods by an old man of the tribe to be initiated into manhood. There he stayed for a number of days. He fasted, smeared himself with dirt and ashes, plunged into ice-cold water, and bruised himself by bashing into rocks. The old man observed him, hoping to identify Hiawatha's guardian spirit—the force that would guide him through life.

During this time, Hiawatha was to pay particular attention to his dreams and report them to the old man, who recognized any visits by spirits. Perhaps it was these dreams that led Hiawatha to become a medicine man. Once the path was chosen, however, he had much to learn.

Hiawatha first learned that there were three causes of illness: natural causes, such as wounds, broken bones, and frostbite; evil spirits; and sorcery, or some powerful person's magic. To treat the three types of illness, the tribes had three kinds of medicine men: surgeon-physicians, priests, and magicians. Sometimes one man had knowledge of all the types of medicine. These elders taught Hiawatha how to clean and dress a wound, which medicines to use to treat different problems, and how to make poultices, ointments, and teas from herbs, roots, and berries. They also showed him how to set broken bones and splint them with bark or wood.

Next Hiawatha mastered the mystical knowledge of dreams so that he could diagnose spiritual illnesses. He had to memorize long songs and complicated rituals and be able to perform them perfectly. If his performance was right, he could restore harmony with the unseen spirits and heal a patient. If the patient didn't recover and there was no explanation, then sorcery might be the cause of the illness. Sorcery was much more difficult to deal with than a broken bone or a spiritual illness.

Hiawatha listened carefully to his teachers and thought about what they said. His wisdom, his success at helping people, and his sincere love for fellow beings made him well known and respected among all the Iroquois people. By talking and listening to the many people who came to see him, Hiawatha became familiar with their desires, hopes, and fears. As he understood the difficulty of their lives and the grief caused by the constant raids and revenge, Hiawatha wanted to do more than just heal their bodies. He wanted to heal their way of life.

While Hiawatha was growing up, he did not understand the terrible life his people had. Probably very few adults realized how bad things were, since no one could imagine any other way of life. For years the Onondagas, Cayugas, Oneidas, Mohawks,

and Senecas had continually raided each other's villages, burning houses and cornfields, killing, torturing, and sometimes
eating their victims! And now the Onondagas lived in fear of
one of their own warrior chiefs.

Outside the largest Onondaga village, near the one in
which Hiawatha grew up, lived a man the Onondagas called
Atotarho, which means "tangled." Atotarho was crafty, jealous,
intelligent, and fearful to behold. Although he was a sachem, he
did not attend the tribal councils. Instead he stayed in his own
lodge in a dark ravine and slept on a bed of bulrushes. Some
people even claimed that he ate men and women raw!

Atotarho was so wicked that people in other villages,
remembering stories they had heard, claimed he had snakes
instead of hair coming out of his head. Many believed he was a
sorcerer, and brave men were so afraid of his piercing stare and
stern face that their knees buckled and they went speechless in
his presence.

Almost all the Onondagas were afraid of Atotarho, and
dared not speak out against him, even secretly. Those who did
were often found dead of unknown causes, or they mysteriously
disappeared. But Atotarho didn't need supernatural power to
accomplish these things. He easily manipulated the men who
surrounded him. He fooled some into thinking he was supernatural; others he bribed; some he simply threatened. However
he controlled them, they would do anything Atotarho asked of
them. They were his spies—reporting whatever they heard by
listening at doorways and hiding behind trees. Then they acted
as his agents, doing whatever he ordered, even when it included
murder.

No member of the Onondagas knew how Atotarho became
so powerful. Normally, the Iroquois would not have put up with
such a tyrant. Within their villages, most Iroquois had a very
orderly way of life. Inside their longhouse, Hiawatha's mother,

father, brothers, and sisters shared one of several firesides. The other firesides in their longhouse belonged to the families of his mother's sisters and cousins. The longhouse now belonged to his grandmother. She, her sisters, and her female cousins (who had their own longhouses in the village) chose the sachems who governed the tribe. Usually, if they were not good sachems, the same matrons who chose them had them removed. But it was usually the war chief who was sent to remove the offending sachem, and Atotarho himself was the war chief. In addition, he was such an effective warrior that the Onondagas probably thought they needed him to ward off their enemies.

No matter why they tolerated him, the Onondagas were helpless prisoners. They lived in constant fear, afraid of their neighbors, but even more afraid of the enemy within.

5

Marriage

In Atotarho's village lived a beautiful young woman, Tonedawa. Hiawatha's mother had known Tonedawa's mother when they were both children, so she was pleased when the woman approached her to suggest the marriage of her daughter to Hiawatha. Hiawatha's marriage was not based on love but on practical considerations. After the two mothers had agreed, they announced the forthcoming marriage in the longhouses.

It was the custom among the Onondagas for the mothers to arrange marriages for their children. It was also the custom that one could only marry someone from a different clan. Clans were groups of people who shared the same *totem*, or animal symbol, such as a bear, wolf, or turtle. The *emblem*, or crest, of the clan was always displayed over the

An artist's impression of Hiawatha's marriage

two entrances of the longhouse. Among the Iroquois, members of the same clan were never allowed to marry. They were considered to be brothers and sisters, even though they might be distant cousins or related only by adoption or even members of different tribes. A member of the bear clan of the Mohawks, for example, could not marry a member of the Onondaga bear clan.

On the day of her wedding, Tonedawa dressed in doeskin, put wooden combs in her hair, and walked with her mother through the forest to Hiawatha's village. The two women were welcomed at the gate by the children of Hiawatha's clan. His sisters, curious about the bride, watched from the distance. The mothers exchanged gifts in the longhouse of Hiawatha's family.

Tonedawa's mother gave the groom's mother thick cakes of unleavened corn bread. In return, Hiawatha's mother gave dried venison to the mother of the bride.

After a time, Hiawatha gathered his bow and arrows, his medicine basket, and clothing, and bade his family goodbye. In this matriarchal society, it was the custom for a man to go to live in the longhouse of his wife's family. This was a sad moment for Hiawatha. He had lived his entire life in this longhouse. Now it would no longer be his home. His heart was very heavy as he walked through the gate of his village. The little wedding party—bride, groom, and mother of the bride—walked single file, with a few of Hiawatha's cousins and brothers trailing behind.

Hiawatha, usually an eloquent speaker, had little to say to his bride as they walked through the woods. He had not talked much with women since that last day he had gone to the corn-field with his mother so long ago. He had spent all his time—even mealtime—with men and boys. Although women prepared the food, they did not eat with the men.

When the wedding party arrived at the bride's village, Hiawatha noticed that the same aromas lingered as in his village. The longhouse, too, looked much the same. Ears of dry corn, tied together by their husks, hung inside. The sleeping benches were lined with fur, and beneath them were clay pots filled with corn and beans from the last harvest. And the hospitality was the same. Hiawatha was barely through the door before his new family offered him food.

The wedding party walked the length of the longhouse. Hiawatha met his new aunts, uncles, and cousins, and finally Tonedawa's grandmother, the matron, who led them to their new hearth. With the lighting of the hearth fire, Hiawatha and Tonedawa were married.

In time the two strangers grew to love and trust each other. In spring, at the time of the Strawberry Festival, their first daughter was born. The next year, they had another daughter, and the next year another. When their seventh daughter was born, Tonedawa told Hiawatha that a man should have a son. He said, "We need no more warriors."

As his daughters grew, he was very pleased with them. They were strong and beautiful. His only wish was that their lives could be better. The Onondagas were now living in an almost continual state of war.

One year Hiawatha had watched the women of the village work all spring and summer tending their cornfield. The corn grew tall, with squash and bean vines winding around the stalks. One night, when the harvest was near, a party of Senecas came out of the woods and burned the field. The village might have starved if it hadn't been for the generosity of other Onondaga villages and a supply of grain saved from the year before. Still it was a very hard winter for them.

Hiawatha watched the young women of the longhouse become widows almost as fast as he had seen them become married. If their young husbands were not killed in battle, they were soon hardened by the brutality of war. Boys who had once laughed as they played snow snake became men who never smiled.

To make things worse, Hiawatha had somehow attracted Atotarho's rage. Some people thought Atotarho's anger grew from jealousy. Hiawatha was a wise medicine man and by now a high-ranking sachem, respected by the whole tribe. He was an eloquent speaker, who easily won people to his side of an argument. Others thought Atotarho might have hated Hiawatha for even deeper reasons. Atotarho believed warfare was the only way to avoid being wiped out. On the other hand, Hiawatha believed the only way for human beings to avoid destroying themselves was to put down their weapons. But without strife, Atotarho, the war chief, could not maintain his own power.

The longer Hiawatha lived, the more he wondered why the customs of the longhouse could not be extended from village to village, from tribe to tribe. In the longhouse, each family lived by its own fireside with its own tools, clothing, and personal items, but all the longhouse families worked together to grow and harvest food and hunt. Then they all shared whatever they had.

Of course things were not always perfect in the long-houses. Husbands and wives quarreled. Rivalries developed. Some people didn't do their share of the work. Whenever troubles arose that could not be settled within the longhouse, the clan chiefs were asked to call a council and settle the matter. Hiawatha thought a system that worked within the longhouse should work with all people.

The more he thought about it, the more it seemed possible to work out a lasting peace among the tribes. When he brought his idea to the tribal council, the other chiefs waited patiently for him to finish; then they responded.

"You are a wise and good man, Hiawatha," said one, "but you may be too young to remember when the Onondagas joined with the Mohawks to defeat the Hurons. We sat with their chiefs around the council fire and smoked tobacco together. They were good men. But after the Hurons were driven back, a Mohawk youth, hunting rabbits far from his village, was crushed by a boulder. The matron of his longhouse dreamed that two Onondaga warriors had pushed the boulder from its perch. She sent a war party to capture an Onondaga youth. The peace was over between us."

Hiawatha listened as each of the chiefs told a similar story. When they had finished, he said, "All these things you speak of are true. That is why we need to make a new kind of league. In the past, when we have joined with other tribes, we have only done so to fight a common enemy. We did not become true brothers and sisters. We had no rules to live by after the trouble had passed."

Hiawatha explained that he envisioned a great council fire, surrounded by chiefs from all the nations, chosen by their own people. "The Great Council would settle disputes between tribes, just as our council settles disputes between clans. Surely, if twelve families can live peacefully together under one long-house roof, and twelve longhouses can stand beside each other within the walls of a village, then twelve nations can live in peace under the great roof of the stars."

One chief said, "I don't want Senecas telling us what to do." Another said it was difficult enough to settle problems in one's own village without outsiders interfering.

Hiawatha said, "We could leave tribal matters to the tribes and village matters to the village. Cayugas would still be Cayugas, and Onondagas would still be Onondagas. We would just work out better ways to settle our disputes so that we'd no longer have to kill each other to get justice. The killing never stops. A Cayuga kills one of our people. We get revenge by killing one of theirs, but we also kill two more to keep from being killed. On and on it goes."

The other chiefs looked at Hiawatha and at each other as though lightning had just struck one of the nearby trees. As terrible as the consequences were, what other way was there to make up for the death of a beloved son or daughter? How else could the loss of a wife or husband be avenged?

"Nothing is as valuable as a human life," replied Hia-watha, "but I have never seen the taking of one life restore another."

Hiawatha believed the only hope for human beings was to find an answer to the problem of revenge. He was certain that a permanent union of all Indian nations would bring about the peace of the longhouse. He decided to start with his own tribe and called a meeting of all the chiefs and people of the Onondaga nation. Because he was so highly respected, many came.

Many years later, an Onondaga chief repeated the story of that meeting, saying, "They came together from along the creeks, from all parts, to the general council fire."

Unfortunately, Atotarho was one of those who came, along with his spies. One legend says that Atotarho tricked some who were canoeing across a wide spot in the river to attend the meeting. Watching them from the shore, he shouted, "Look out! Look out! Stand up and look behind you. A storm is coming and you will be overturned!" Many people panicked and stood up in their canoes to look around for the storm. In fact, a stormy wind did seem to start blowing at that moment. The movement of the wind and all the people standing up caused most of the canoes to overturn, and many people drowned. The few who escaped no longer wanted to have a meeting.

Even without such a tragedy, once Atotarho appeared the meeting was doomed. No one was willing to talk openly. The failure of the first meeting didn't discourage Hiawatha; he called a second one.

This time fewer people came from the distant villages. Again Atotarho appeared and broke up the meeting. Still Hiawatha did not give up. He called a third meeting. This time, however, no one attended, and Hiawatha's spirit was crushed. He sat for a long time with his head bowed, covered by a mantle of skins, as though he were in mourning. According to some accounts, it was after this failure that Hiawatha gathered his few possessions and left the Onondagas, becoming a lone wanderer.

Legend

Another legend told among the Iroquois
claims that Hiawatha first became a wanderer because of great personal sorrow.
Again Atotarho was to blame. The
legend goes that Atotarho was not satisfied merely
to defeat Hiawatha's plan; he wished to destroy
Hiawatha and his entire family, one by one. He
used one of the evil men in his service, a powerful
medicine man named Osinoh, to carry out his plan.
On the appointed night Osinoh followed Atotarho's
instructions.

At that time, Hiawatha lived with Tonedawa
and his daughters in a *lodge*, a smaller and more
private dwelling, surrounded by woods. Osinoh
climbed into the trees that overlooked the roof hole,
concealing himself among the leaves. He filled his

mouth with clay and imitated the sound of a screech owl. Calling out the name of Hiawatha's youngest daughter, he said, "Unless you marry Osinoh, you will die. Whoo-whoo." Then he climbed down and went to his own house.

The next morning Hiawatha's daughter told her mother about hearing the screech owl call out her name. Crying, she said, "I don't want to marry Osinoh, Mother. He is ugly and cruel."

Her mother said, "Don't worry. I will decide who you are to marry, and it will not be Osinoh. You can be certain of that."

Within a few days the daughter became very sick. Hiawatha tried every kind of medicine he knew to cure her, but nothing worked. In three days she died.

Hiawatha and Tonedawa were miserable. To show their grief, they covered themselves in furs and lay on the floor with their faces in the ashes of their hearth, as was the custom. They didn't eat or drink. Relatives wrapped the girl in furs and fashioned a bark coffin for her. Even before she was buried in the village cemetery, whispers went from longhouse to longhouse that Hiawatha's daughter had been killed by Atotarho. Fearing for themselves, people avoided the grieving family.

Hiawatha and his family had barely ended their period of mourning when Osinoh returned, again climbing into the tree and filling his mouth with clay. This time he called out the name of the next youngest daughter.

"Unless you marry Osinoh, you will die. Whoo-whoo," he said.

When the daughter went to her mother the next morning, Tonedawa was afraid. She remembered that the same thing had happened shortly before her youngest daughter had become sick. Although she told her daughter not to worry, that she would never have to marry Osinoh, Tonedawa still feared

Atotarho's sorcery. She talked with Hiawatha of her fears, and he burned some cleansing herbs in the house. But he felt sick at heart. He did not know how to deal with hatred and sorcery. Within a day or two his daughter also sickened and died. Again the family mourned and buried its dead. Now no one came near them; they were all afraid of Atotarho.

One by one each of the daughters died in the same way, until only the eldest daughter and Tonedawa remained. The three of them lived in a perpetual state of fear and sorrow. Hiawatha could see no beauty anywhere. When he looked at the stars they looked like tears.

Atotarho

The people of Tonedawa's clan wanted to help. Every night the men of the old longhouse stationed themselves outside Hiawatha's lodge, hiding themselves in the shadows. They didn't know what to expect or what they could do but they waited, armed with their bows and arrows and war clubs.

On the seventh night that Osinoh climbed the tree, there was no moon. The men guarding the house could not even see their own feet. They didn't know Osinoh was there until they heard him call out Tonedawa's name.

"Unless you marry Osinoh," he sang, "you will die. Whoo-whoo."

As Osinoh climbed down from the trees, one of Tonedawa's cousins shot him with an arrow. Osinoh fell to the ground; the cousin rushed forward with a club to kill the evil man. But Osinoh looked up at him calmly and said, "You cannot club me. Your arm has no power at all. It weakens. Today I shall recover from this wound. It will do you no good to injure me further."

Everything happened exactly as Osinoh said. Tonedawa's cousin could not lift his club. Osinoh went home and his wound healed. Tonedawa fell ill and in three days she died just as her daughters had.

After Tonedawa's death, Hiawatha lay wrapped in furs with his head in the ashes of his cold hearth, refusing all food and drink. He stayed this way until he himself was near death. Finally, his eldest daughter came and sat beside him.

"Father," she said, "it is time for you to walk among the living." Hiawatha said nothing.

His daughter sat silently for a moment, then said, "You are going to have a grandchild."

Hiawatha stirred very slightly. After a while he reached out his hand to his daughter and said, "From the ashes of death comes the hope of a new life."

Not long afterward, Hiawatha emerged from his house of mourning. He called for a meeting of the clan. When they gathered he said, "Some of you have avoided me in fear of evoking Atotarho's wrath. I don't blame you. Even I have thought that I should leave you, as if the hatred would follow me out of the village. Now, however, I have come to tell you that the hatred will remain behind."

Elders of the clan took turns speaking. "We must no longer turn our backs, pretending not to see," said one, "while Atotarho works his evil."

"As long as Atotarho lives among us, no one will ever be safe," agreed another.

"We must call a tribal council."

"How can we do that? If Atotarho hears of it, he won't allow it."

"Atotarho will not hear of it if no one tells him. We can have a secret meeting, inviting only those we most trust."

"How can we know whom to trust, when Atotarho's spies are everywhere?"

"We must take the chance. We must stand up to Atotarho now or he will destroy us all in the end."

Word of the meeting was passed along secretly from one person to the next. There was, however, no way to keep such a thing from Atotarho. It was just a matter of time before an informer crept to the cruel chief's lodge and told him about the plan. When he heard, Atotarho said, "How dare they turn against me! It is I who protect them from their enemies. Don't they know by now how powerful I am?"

He looked at the informer for a moment and said, "I had meant to show mercy to Hiawatha by sparing his last daughter and her unborn child. But now I will make the 'great peacemaker' a living example of what I do to those who plot against me."

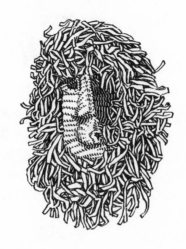

Husk face mask

On the day of the meeting, people assembled at the appointed place and waited for Hiawatha to come. When he arrived, his daughter was with him, but she soon wandered off to gather sticks for the council fire. Suddenly, Atotarho emerged from the forest and stood for a moment looking at the crowd as though he wanted to remember every face that was there. Then he looked at the sky and began to point.

"A beautiful creature is falling," he shouted. Everyone looked up to see a bird plummeting to earth as though shot by an arrow. Its beautiful feathers, which were much prized by the Onondagas, were showering down in the clearing, and the crowd rushed to pick them up as they fell.

In their eagerness to grab the feathers that were falling from the sky, they didn't see Hiawatha's daughter. They knocked her to the ground and trampled her to death while Hiawatha stood, helpless.

After that, the story goes, Hiawatha left the Onondagas and became a solitary wanderer.

7

The Wanderer

Hiawatha left his home behind. Hundreds of years later, Skanawati, the Onondaga sachem, repeated a story handed down to him about Hiawatha. Half-crazy with grief, Hiawatha went from lodge to lodge among the Onondagas, looking for help. But no one would take him in. People said kind things to him, but they were afraid to take on more trouble than they already had—and they were afraid of Atotarho.

An old Onondaga, famous for his dreams, had once predicted that Hiawatha would go to live among the Mohawks, where he would meet a great man. Together they would overcome Atotarho. That prophecy, and strange stories Hiawatha had heard of a mysterious man named Dekanawida, caused him to turn east toward the land of the Mohawks.

Hiawatha wandered for many days, through woods, over mountains, across a lake—always in the direction of the sunrise—until at last he came to the land of the Mohawks. After being turned away from every Onondaga hearth, Hiawatha had decided that human beings were basically bad. By now he expected nothing from the Mohawks and Dekanawida. He remembered how his own kind had abandoned him, only coming to his side when they finally realized that they themselves were in danger. He believed there would never be peace among human beings. People were too selfish and uncaring. So he built a hut of hemlock boughs and lived as a hermit deep in the woods. He ate mostly berries, nuts, and tubers, killing what game he could.

During his journey, he had found some beautiful white shells along the shore of a lake and now, with little else to do, he fashioned them into the tubular beads called *wampum*. As he strung them together on leather thongs, he kept thinking about the terrible problem of revenge: a life for a life. There could be no peace as long as revenge continued.

As Hiawatha put bead after bead on a string, he thought how much people valued wampum. They gave it as gifts and sometimes used it for trade. Why wouldn't it be possible, he wondered, to buy one's own life and pay for another with wampum instead of blood? The more he thought about it, the more reasonable it seemed. But then, of course, everyone would have to agree. They would have to admit that no amount of killing could restore a life. They also would have to agree that survivors should be compensated to discourage them from seeking revenge. These ideas went around and around in Hiawatha's head until he had worked out a plan.

It wasn't long before a band of Mohawk boys roaming the forest spotted the smoke from Hiawatha's fire and hurried back to their village to report it. The Mohawks quickly sent a scout to find out where the smoke was coming from. The scout hid in the trees and watched the hut. He was surprised to see what appeared to be an Onondaga sachem come out of the hut, sit down, and start sewing like a woman. The scout moved closer. The Onondaga wasn't sewing after all but stringing beads.

Hiawatha could not see the scout, but he could feel the man's presence. He said, "I am Hiawatha. I have come from over the mountain. I mean you no harm."

Hiawatha knew that Mohawks were very hospitable to other Mohawks but they didn't hesitate to torture and kill strangers. Hiawatha hoped that his name had meaning to the person hiding in the woods.

The scout raced back to the village to report what he had seen and heard.

The next day Hiawatha was visited by two Mohawk men—a sachem and a medicine man—who seemed to materialize out of the forest. Hiawatha welcomed them and offered them dried venison, which they accepted.

After a while the sachem spoke. "If you are truly Hiawatha, sachem of the Onondagas, why are you here in the land of the Mohawks?"

"I don't know why I've come. My moccasins brought me here," Hiawatha said. "Perhaps I have come to die, or because it was dreamed that I should. I have heard of a great being who lives among you. Perhaps that is why I have come, to meet a wise man."

Hiawatha paused. There was silence, except for the wind in the treetops. "If you had asked me instead to say why I have left my own country, I would say that Atotarho has destroyed it, sparing only hatred and fear."

Again the three men sat without talking. Then the Mohawk medicine man said, "We have heard of the prophecy. It is whispered across the land that Dekanawida and Hiawatha together will overcome Atotarho." He paused. "I have heard that Atotarho has snakes for hair and that his body is bent in a terrible way. Is that true?"

Hiawatha answered, "His hair is snarled and filthy, but it is not his body that is twisted; it is his soul."

The medicine man said, "I have also heard that Atotarho is a cannibal." He waited for Hiawatha to reply.

Hiawatha looked at the ground. He had heard that the Mohawks themselves were cannibals. "Atotarho would enjoy knowing that people believe he eats his enemies. Such rumors make him stronger."

Finally, it was Hiawatha's turn to ask questions. "Who is this man you call Dekanawida?"

The sachem said, "Some say he was sent to us by the Creator. He came to us out of the north, from far across the lake, paddling a white canoe. Later, people said his canoe was made of stone. Yet it did not sink but skimmed over the water." The sachem paused, to be sure Hiawatha understood how remarkable the canoe was.

"Dekanawida's birth itself was said to have been miraculous," the sachem continued. "But who knows. The story goes that his mother, Jigonsasee, lived with her own mother in a lodge beside a lake, far from the nearest village. They had no relatives and no one visited. Jigonsasee was a quiet and obedient daughter. It is said she never went out without her mother. Yet soon after she reached womanhood, she became pregnant.

"Her mother, Lagentci, was shocked and furious. 'Who is the father?' she demanded. Jigonsasee replied, 'Mother, please believe me. I don't know how this happened.'

"But Lagentci did not believe her," said the sachem, "and from then on she mistreated Jigonsasee, scolding her, insulting her, and even beating her. When Jigonsasee's time drew near, her mother had a long dream. In the dream a man appeared and told Lagentci to stop grieving and to stop treating her daughter so badly. It was the wish of the Creator to have Jigonsasee bring to earth a male child who would have a great mission in the world. This child would be called Dekanawida." The sachem was silent.

Then the medicine man spoke. "Others say the grandmother's dream also predicted that Dekanawida would bring about the destruction of his people. They say that when the child was born, the grandmother became frightened and angry. While Jigonsasee was asleep, Lagentci took the infant out of the house and down to the frozen lake, where she tried to drown him. But the next morning the baby appeared, happy and well, in his mother's arms. The next day Lagentci again took the baby while Jigonsasee slept, went to the shore of the lake, and threw

him into the icy water. When she returned to the lodge, she found Jigonsasee nursing her newborn baby. After that the grandmother knew that she must let the infant live. She didn't try to harm Dekanawida again."

Hiawatha listened intently, thinking about the significance of the stories. "Why did Dekanawida come to live among the Mohawks?" he asked.

The medicine man answered, "It was his destiny. His people, the Hurons, shunned him as they would any fatherless child. Some thought the grandmother had made up the dream, and so they didn't believe the Creator had sent him. Some believed he was dangerous, because of the evil prophecy.

"As Dekanawida grew up," the medicine man continued, "he never went into the forest with the other boys to hunt and learn the ways of manhood. Instead he stayed with his mother, who talked with him about the evils of war. When he should have been thinking about killing his first deer, he was thinking instead about a family of nations."

Hiawatha could not believe what he was hearing. For a moment he felt hope!

The medicine man went on. "He had such a passion for spiritual matters—peace and noble deeds—that by the time he was ready to mingle with the people in the village, he could talk of little else. Worse yet, whenever he got excited, he stammered! Those who didn't disappear when they saw him coming would openly mock him."

Hiawatha's thoughts again turned dark. It was pointless to dream of a good world when people themselves were so worthless.

"A lesser person," said the medicine man, "would have retreated or would have tried to learn to talk about things that interested others. But Dekanawida was not an ordinary youth.

He was as good as he was handsome. His natural intelligence and sensitivity created in him a spirit of calmness and power. The people saw that he endured their taunts and tricks without losing his temper. Some of those who had tormented him learned to love him and began to admit that life would be sweet indeed without the bitterness of war."

The medicine man continued, "One day Dekanawida had walked deep into the forest, asking himself what was the purpose of all his talk of peace. Hadn't sensible people always wanted peace? Was he really saying anything new? It was easy, he thought, to make war, but how do human beings make peace?

"Then," said the medicine man, "in the dark of the forest, a vision swept over him. He saw a spruce tree, so tall that its upper branches went right through the skies. The tree had four great white roots, stretching out in the four directions of the Earth. Beneath the tree lay a snow-white carpet of thistledown, spreading out to protect the land. At the top of the tree was perched an eagle. The tree was called the Tree of Peace. It drew its nourishment from three double principles. Without these, the tree would die." The medicine man fell silent.

Hiawatha questioned, "What were these three double principles?"

The medicine man said, "Dekanawida can explain them better. However, I will tell you this. In order for a whole nation to be healthy, the people in it must be healthy in both mind and spirit; but, if the people are to be healthy, their nation must be healthy. Next, people must agree to obey the laws; but the laws must be just, and disobedience must be punished in a fair way. Finally, there must be a way to defend the tribe; to do that well, the tribe must have a strong spirit, which comes from the strong spirit of its members . . ."

Hiawatha said, "I will have to think about what you have said. I don't understand all of it."

The medicine man said, "Dekanawida could make you see the wisdom of these things."

The sachem said, "After his great vision, Dekanawida knew it was time to go out into the world with his message of peace. That was when he crossed the water in his canoe, which people said was made of stone."

The three men sat silently for a long time. Then Hiawatha picked up a string of pure white wampum. Handing it to the sachem, he said, "Here, take this to Dekanawida and let it speak to him of peace. Let it tell him that Hiawatha awaits him."

8

The Meeting of Hiawatha and Dekanawida

A few days after the two Mohawks had visited him, Hiawatha was sitting in front of his hut, stringing his white wampum. He was deep in thought when suddenly he felt another human presence. He looked up. Standing before him was a tall, silver-haired man whose face was handsome and gentle.

"I am Dekanawida," he said. "I received your gift of peace, younger brother. Now I bring you a gift of sympathy, for I have heard of your great sorrow, and these are my tears."

After Hiawatha welcomed Dekanawida's gift of purple wampum, the two men sat silently facing each other. Then Hiawatha said, "I once dreamed as you do of peace among nations, but I have come to see that it will never happen. We will go on killing each other until only one warrior remains. And when he dies, old and alone, and his bones are picked clean, then at last there will be peace."

Dekanawida said, "Your sorrow speaks, Hiawatha, not you."

"I was such a fool," Hiawatha said. "I thought the whole world could be one longhouse, a family of families. But it cannot be."

"For what reasons?" Dekanawida asked.

Hiawatha said, "Because there will always be Atotarhos among us, those who are sick with evil and cause trouble."

"Then that is the starting point," said Dekanawida. "We must work to improve each human being before we can improve the nation. That is the first of the three double principles that nourish the great Tree of Peace that stands at the center of the Earth. What else keeps us from gathering together under the Tree of Peace?"

"Revenge!" cried Hiawatha. "As long as human beings kill each other and others take revenge we cannot live in peace."

"All of us are scarred. No one has been untouched by these wars," Dekanawida said. "What can be done to stop them?"

Hiawatha answered, "I have been thinking about this very question. It is wrong to kill, and it is useless to take revenge, yet justice requires that something be done."

Then Hiawatha told Dekanawida his thoughts about wampum. "Instead of taking revenge, the victim's family would receive a certain number of shell strings for each person killed. And the killer would have to purchase his own life as well!"

Dekanawida said, "That is a good plan, Hiawatha. You say there is no hope of peace, yet you have shown a way to bring about the second double principle. It is this: The people must do what is right, but when they do wrong, all parties must receive justice."

Then Dekanawida asked, "What else prevents us from living peacefully together?"

Hiawatha pondered this question for a very long time. When he thought of the answer, it disturbed him.

"Outsiders," he answered at last. "Even if all our nations came together as one, someday crooked tongues would come from over the mountain or across the river to destroy us. We would need to be able, in both body and spirit, to protect what was rightfully ours. We would have to stand together as one family."

"And that is the third double principle," Dekanawida said. "You already know what I saw in my vision of the Tree of Peace." Then he went on to explain how the three double principles might be put into practice.

Dekanawida had worked out a great plan, based on the unwritten laws of the longhouse. He would not establish new laws but refine the old ones, which would then apply to all the nations that joined a league. Dekanawida did not want to change the basic society, which he believed was good; he only wanted to keep it from being destroyed.

After Hiawatha had heard all of Dekanawida's plan, the two of them sat listening to the wind song of the trees.

Finally, Hiawatha said, "There is great wisdom in all of this, but how can it be passed on to others? We have seen how stories change each time they are told. If these laws are to bring peace among us, they cannot be changed in every mouth."

Dekanawida thought about what Hiawatha had said. "Men will learn the laws the same way medicine men learn their songs. They will repeat them until they cannot forget them. And when these men grow old, they will pass the laws on to younger men, who will then commit them to memory. This way our people will never again forget how to live."

Hiawatha said, "It would take a very long time to learn what you have told me. If one person made a mistake, the law would be changed. Soon we would have no law at all. Tribes would quarrel about how many sachems they could send to the council. People would quarrel about the proper color of wampum to give."

Dekanawida said, "There is a way."

Hiawatha sat looking at the strings of purple wampum Dekanawida had given him and thought about his strings of white wampum. Each color had a different meaning. White was sacred and signified peace and nurturing, which was the feminine side of life. Purple represented the masculine side of life—hunting, war, and sometimes death. But the purple that Dekanawida had given him also signified sympathy.

Hiawatha remembered a piece of clothing his mother made long ago. It was decorated with quill beads, sewn in many rows. The design had reminded him of something.

"That looks like a tree," he had said.

"Then let it be a tree," she had answered.

Hiawatha could still hear his mother's voice. Suddenly, he said, "We could put the words into the beads." He arranged some of his white, unstrung beads on the ground. "Here is your Tree of Peace," he said to Dekanawida, "and here is the white carpet. Here are antlers to represent a sachem."

Dekanawida thought for a long time. He closed his eyes and sang a song, rocking back and forth slowly. "Yes," he said at last, "then the words would not change with the wind."

They both sat thinking, saying nothing, until Hiawatha said, "Words are not enough. Even with your true vision, there can be no great council fire, no Tree of Peace, as long as Atotarho lives."

"It is true," said Dekanawida, "that there is no hope if Atotarho remains as he is now—vicious, filled with rage, jealous of power. But remember the first double principle: We must improve each human being before we can improve a nation. Atotarho must be made well; then he will no longer oppose what is good. Have you forgotten, Hiawatha, that you are a great medicine man?"

Hiawatha felt a great surge of anger. When it was gone, he answered, "Why would I do for my enemy what I could not do for any of my seven daughters or my beloved wife?"

Dekanawida stood up and said, "If you heal Atotarho, you will also heal yourself, now so sick with grief and bitterness."

When he saw that his guest was ready to return to the village, Hiawatha stood and wished him a safe journey. They would need to meet many times before they had a plan. They would present it first to the Mohawk sachems. If the Mohawks agreed, Hiawatha would consider approaching Atotarho. In the meantime, Hiawatha would need time to think and to heal.

Dekanawida and Hiawatha worked together until they were ready to meet with a Mohawk council. The council began with the sachems passing a *calumet*, or ceremonial pipe, so that the tobacco smoke might rise and carry their hope for peace into the heavens. Because Dekanawida stammered whenever he tried to speak in public, he asked Hiawatha to present the plan.

The Mohawks raised the same questions that leaders of Hiawatha's own village had raised. But the Mohawks had suffered even more from the raids than had the Onondagas, so they were desperate for change.

Hiawatha explained the plan as it then stood. "There will be one Great Council, made up of sachems from every nation that joins. Each nation, village, clan, and longhouse will manage its own affairs, just as it does now, but no nation will war against another. Instead nations will take their grievances to the Great Council for settlement." Hiawatha paused, waiting for questions.

"Suppose that someone has come in the night and murdered my daughter and son as they sleep? What can your Great Council do about that?" the first sachem asked.

Hiawatha said, "Nothing. No number of sachems from all the nations of the world could give you back your son and daughter. But neither would your children be returned to you if you killed the murderer's own family."

The sachems looked at each other, and Hiawatha continued. "Under the plan, the murderer would have to pay you thirty strings of wampum for your loss, ten for your son and twenty for your daughter. He also would have to pay you another twenty strings not to kill him."

The sachem said, "What good would wampum be to me? Would it heal my broken spirit?"

"No," Hiawatha said, "but it would keep you from becoming the cowardly killer of some other children who are lying asleep. Would such an act heal your spirit?"

The sachem said nothing. The only sound was the crackle of the council fire. Then he asked, "Why only ten strings for my son and twenty for my daughter? Don't they both love life the same?"

Hiawatha said, "Yes. They would both wish to grow old before traveling to the beautiful Forest Beyond the Red Lakes of the Sunset. The price is not based on how much they value their own lives; it is based on the needs of their family. The Creator made women the guardians of life. They plant the fields and bear the children. They rule the longhouse. Without women there could be no nation." And then he added quietly, "Without men there could be no war."

After a time another sachem said, "What do you suppose Atotarho would say to this? Imagine the sachems of the Great Council of nations going to Atotarho and saying, 'You owe the Cayugas forty strings of wampum for the warriors you killed.' What do you think would happen? He would laugh a terrible laugh. Then he would spit on the ground," the sachem said. "And who would go to him with such a proposition? Who is strong enough?"

Hiawatha answered, "The law is strong enough. As an Onondaga sachem, he would be a member of the Great Council and obliged to uphold the laws that the nations agree upon. If he failed to do this, his women relatives would have him removed, and the whole council would back them up."

The first sachem who had spoken said, "What makes you think Atotarho would join the Great Council in the first place?"

"Because it would benefit him," Hiawatha said.

"In what way?"

"In this way," Hiawatha explained. "A single arrow breaks easily, but that same arrow bound together with others becomes strong. Atotarho devotes much of his time to terrorizing his own people into following him. If the other nations were united against him, he would only be one arrow. Soon he would be broken."

When Hiawatha had finished, the sachems spoke.

"If you persuade the Onondagas to join, others will follow," said one. "If you don't, there can be no peace."

"Yes," agreed another. "The Mohawks wish to live in peace with all their brothers."

"Hiawatha, if you convince Atotarho to sit with us at the council fire," said a third, "we will welcome you as a Mohawk."

9
Making Alliances

Hiawatha and Dekanawida set out to persuade the neighboring Iroquois nations to join the Mohawks under the Tree of Peace. In the forest just west of the Mohawks, and north, toward the head of what is now called the Mohawk River, lived the Oneidas. Just as Hiawatha had approached the Mohawks with care, he and Dekanawida stopped a short distance from the Oneida village. They built a shelter and made a fire to signal their presence. Just as the Mohawks had sent a scout, so did the Oneidas. Within a day or so a party of wary Oneidas came to meet the strangers. Dekanawida and Hiawatha sent strings of white wampum to their principal sachem. In time the two men were invited to his lodge, where they met with him and other village sachems.

The Oneidas listened with interest to the plan, asking some of the same questions the Mohawks had. But they were more concerned about how much power the Mohawks would have than they were about Atotarho. Atotarho had never bothered them; the Mohawks did, however, with continual raids.

One of the sachems said, "The Mohawk nation is very large, larger than the Oneida nation. Does that mean the Mohawks will have more say at the Great Council fires?"

Dekanawida and Hiawatha talked with each other for a moment. Then Hiawatha answered, "No, all nations will be equal at the council fire. Each will have only one vote. However, each nation will be represented by more than one sachem. The bigger the nation, the more sachems they will have. But this will not affect their influence at the council fire. All the sachems representing a nation must agree with each other; they must speak with one mind because they only have one vote.

"When we met with the Mohawks, we agreed on fifty sachems altogether," continued Hiawatha. "We have to limit the number or we might end up with too many people around the fire. Then we would never be able to finish our business."

Dekanawida said, "It might even be an advantage to have fewer delegates, because there would be fewer to disagree."

The Oneida sachem persisted. "How many will represent the Mohawks?"

Hiawatha told them what had been agreed upon with the Mohawks, "Nine."

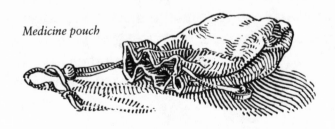

Medicine pouch

"Then there must be nine Oneida sachems," he said, and the others murmured their agreement.

Hiawatha and Dekanawida both said that seemed fair.

One of the Oneidas asked, "What about crooked tongues? What if we are attacked by people who come from the North? If we protect ourselves from them, will we then have to pay wampum for those we kill?"

Hiawatha said, "No, because they would not be under the Tree of Peace. We hope someday that there will be no strangers, that all will be our brothers and sisters; but until then, we would stand with the Oneidas against their enemies."

The principal sachem lit a white calumet and passed it around in the name of peace. Then the sachem spoke. "We like what you have said, but we need to think about it. Come back in one year, and we will tell you the wishes of our people."

Hiawatha and Dekanawida continued their journey, believing the Oneidas would eventually join the alliance. They walked toward Onondaga territory, along the shore of the lake Hiawatha had crossed on his way to the land of the Mohawks. It was spring and the water was high. The beautiful white shells were hidden below the water, but not far from the lakeshore Hiawatha found something that proved to be more valuable than wampum. He found a patch of a certain rare herb that had great healing powers. The two men gathered several plants and put them in Hiawatha's medicine pouch.

The next day Hiawatha led Dekanawida toward the Onondaga village where he had grown to manhood. But even from a distance he could see that it had changed. Much more of the forest had been cleared, and the cornfields he remembered from his childhood were overgrown with weeds and thistle. The outer bark houses were falling down, and some of the fences surrounding the village were missing. Hiawatha didn't have to enter the gate to know that the village had been abandoned by all but a few crows. He knew that his mother's clan and the rest of the village had moved on to find better soil or more abundant water. Hiawatha's mother had been dead for a few years, but the memories were still strong.

He and Dekanawida walked past a row of longhouses until Hiawatha spotted the crest of his mother's clan. "In this place I listened to the stories of my elders, and saw the False Faces flicker in the shadows. Here I watched my mother's nimble fingers turn cornhusks into moccasins and baskets. I wonder what work those fingers do now, in the Forest Beyond the Red Lakes of the Sunset."

The two stayed in the abandoned longhouse that night. Hiawatha slept on the very bench he had slept on as a boy. As he looked through the roof hole at the stars, he wondered how long the great longhouse he and Dekanawida were building would stand—the longhouse that would house and keep safe a family of Iroquois nations.

The next day Hiawatha found the village. It was only half a day's journey from its original site. In the distance, he saw women—his own sisters, cousins, and nieces—working in the cornfield. When he and Dekanawida entered the gate they were greeted by a few old friends, who were surprised and possibly a little frightened to see Hiawatha. The wanderers were invited to the lodge of one of the most important sachems, who was genuinely glad to see Hiawatha. The two travelers offered their gifts of wampum to the sachem. Hiawatha sang a song of good will. When his song was finished, the daughters and wife of the sachem brought bowls of hominy to their guests.

Again Hiawatha told of the plan for the Great Council. The Onondaga sachem said, "Isn't that the same old idea you have been telling us about for years? What makes you think people will accept it now?"

Hiawatha said that it was not just the same old idea, which had been more of a hope than a plan. "Dekanawida," he said, "had a vision in which he saw the Tree of Peace standing at the center of the Earth, a message from the Creator himself."

Dekanawida spoke. He had no trouble telling the details of his vision because he knew them by heart. He never stammered when he repeated what he had memorized. He told the sachem of the four roots and the white carpet made of thistledown. He described the watchful eagle, perched atop the tree.

When Dekanawida had finished, the Onondaga sachem said, "That is surely a vision of the way things should be. But Hiawatha should know better than any other man that Atotarho has not had such a vision. Have you forgotten him, Hiawatha? Or do you suppose he has changed? If anything, he is worse.

"Atotarho's head is so full of evil spirits that he stays in his dark den, away from the sunlight that blinds him and makes him twist with pain. It is said that sometimes, just when he is ready to shoot an arrow, he will drop the bow and his bow arm will hang dead at his side. No medicine society can find the cause. Atotarho is convinced that he has an enemy who is using sorcery on him."

The sachem declared that no one would dare call a council meeting. "No. As long as Atotarho lives, the Onondagas will never join your Great Council."

Disheartened, the two friends left the Onondaga village and headed toward the land of the Cayugas. But the Cayugas had suffered more from Atotarho's cruelty than anyone else.

Their principal sachem said, "Who among the Mohawks and Oneidas could protect us from Atotarho? We would need a strong war chief. Our tribe is small, weakened by years of raids. What you say sounds good, but I am afraid for my people. If we joined, it would only enrage Atotarho."

Hiawatha told him how easily the single arrow breaks and how strong it becomes when it is bound together with others, but the sachem was not easily convinced. "We are too small and weak to survive such an alliance. If Atotarho didn't destroy us, we would be killed by our big brothers," the sachem said.

Hiawatha told him that each nation would have the same power around the council fire—one vote. The sachem quickly responded, "I have heard that the Mohawks and Oneidas would each have nine representatives at the council fire."

"But all of them will come together to cast one vote," Hiawatha said.

The sachem said, "If the Cayugas were to join such an alliance, they would want ten sachems to represent them, so their voice would be loud at the council fire."

After conferring with Dekanawida, Hiawatha said, "If your nation were to join in the Great Council, you could have ten delegates."

The sachem agreed to call a meeting of the Cayuga sachems, but he himself did not want to join unless the Onondagas also promised to lay down their weapons.

After leaving the Cayuga village, Hiawatha and Dekanawida had planned to continue westward toward the land of the Senecas. But both men knew, almost without speaking, that they must turn back toward the Onondagas.

"We cannot bring about the Great Peace without Atotarho," Dekanawida said. "We must find a way."

Hiawatha felt none of the anger he had experienced before when Dekanawida had first suggested that he must heal Atotarho. What the Onondaga sachem had told them about Atotarho stuck with Hiawatha. He thought he might indeed cure Atotarho.

Hiawatha told Dekanawida what he had been thinking. "I think Atotarho drops his bow because his spirit is sick of killing.

Once long ago, I watched a very old medicine man cure a young girl of just such a dead arm. He learned from her dream that her ondinnonk was a clay bowl filled with embers. She was a very good potter, who knew how to make pots that never leaked. But whenever she went with her sisters into the cornfield, her arm died and she could not raise her hoe. The medicine man told her mother to allow the girl to stay at home to work on her pots and bowls, because if there were too few containers, there would be little corn to harvest.

"So," Hiawatha continued, "the girl stayed home and made pots, which she filled with hot coals. Everyone thought she had made too many pots and that they would get in the way. But when the harvest came, every one of them was filled to the brim. The next year was a very bad year. A cloud of locusts came and ate all the corn, even the stalks. But because the pots were filled, the village was saved. After that the girl's arm was healed."

Dekanawida asked, "Did the girl also have headaches that made her twist in pain, as is said of Atotarho?"

"She did not," replied Hiawatha. "But do you remember the herbs I found beside the lake?"

Dekanawida said that of course he did since he had helped Hiawatha gather them.

"They cure just such headaches," Hiawatha said.

🂧🂧🂧🂧🂧 **10** 🂧🂧🂧🂧🂧

The Miraculous Cure

It was a day's journey to Atotarho's village. Hiawatha's head was full of memories. These were the woods he had roamed as a boy. The two men even followed part of the path that Hiawatha and Tonedawa had walked on their wedding day. He remembered going to his wife's village as a stranger, only to find that people there were much the same as they had been in his mother's village. He wondered if Atotarho was like other men he had known.

At last he said out loud, "If Atotarho is not a beast or a demon, he must be a man."

Dekanawida laughed and said, "I can see you are a deep thinker, Hiawatha."

"What I mean to say is that he must want the same things others want, and fear what they fear," explained Hiawatha.

"That seems right," Dekanawida said.

"What if all his killing came about because he believed it was the only way to peace? Perhaps he once believed he could get rid of his enemies or teach them a lesson so they would no longer trouble him," Hiawatha said.

"Then he grew to hate you, because he thought you were aiding his enemies and undermining his power to do what was right," Dekanawida said. "And the more powerful you became, the more vicious he became because he could not remain in control unless people were afraid of him."

"He became like a cruel and stupid uncle who beats his nephews so they will grow up to be good men," Hiawatha said. "His nephews soon learn to sneak around and do things without the uncle's knowledge. Then the uncle becomes angrier still, but now suspicion is added to the anger. Soon the uncle thinks his nephews are always scheming, even when they are asleep beside their mother's hearth."

By the time Dekanawida and Hiawatha walked through the gates of Atotarho's village, they knew how they would approach him. First they went to the longhouse of Tonedawa's clan, where they were welcomed with corncakes and bowls of wild strawberries. When Hiawatha explained their mission, the family had grave doubts.

Tonedawa's mother, now the matron of the longhouse, said, "Perhaps you can forgive him, but I never can. He has taken my very heart from me, eight times over."

But one of Tonedawa's male cousins agreed to carry Hiawatha's message. Hiawatha said, "Take Atotarho these strings of white wampum, which speak of peace and respect among brothers."

Dekanawida added, "Along with the white wampum, carry this purple wampum, as dark as the eagle's wing. Tell Atotarho it speaks of vigilance and strength against our common enemies."

To the surprise of the entire family, the cousin returned just at dusk, reporting that Atotarho would meet with Hiawatha and Dekanawida. "He says that he does not trust the coward Hiawatha, but he wants to know what he is up to."

The next day Hiawatha and Dekanawida went to the ravine where Atotarho had built his lodge. Hiawatha could feel Atotarho's eyes upon him as he and Dekanawida approached. When Hiawatha was sure that Atotarho could see them clearly, he and Dekanawida set up two poles and stretched a line of sinew between them. Then they hung strings of white and purple wampum over the line. Hiawatha sang a song of condolence, as though Atotarho had lost his own children. Afterward, Dekanawida sang a song. Atotarho threw back the buffalo robe that hung over the entrance to his lodge and stood before them, squinting into the light.

They offered him the many strings of wampum, and he received their gift, not quite knowing what else to do. He then offered them pieces of venison, which they accepted. The three of them sat down before the entrance of the lodge. Although Atotarho was alone, Hiawatha knew the forest itself had eyes and ears.

After a long silence, Atotarho spoke. "What errand brings you back to the village you turned your back on, Hiawatha?"

Hiawatha said, "We have come because of a great vision."

Again Dekanawida told of his vision, but this time he emphasized the eagle that sat atop the tree. "The eagle sits poised, ever aware of outside danger. He sees in all directions at once. He is strong and quick to defend peace. Without the eagle, the enemies of those gathered under the Tree of Peace would scatter the gentle ones like rabbits."

Atotarho listened intently. When Dekanawida finished talking about his vision, Hiawatha waited for Atotarho to speak, but Atotarho said nothing.

After a very long silence, Hiawatha spoke. "In the past," he said, "I had foolish ideas that I spread among the people. I imagined that we could form lasting alliances without first having a way to defend ourselves against crooked tongues. I thought if the whole world could be like one longhouse with many families, we would have no need for warriors. Dekanawida has taught me otherwise."

Still Atotarho said nothing. Hiawatha could hear the leaves rustling in the forest and with every sound he imagined one of Atotarho's spies.

Finally the warrior spoke. "I am not the eagle you seek," he said softly. "I am a sick man, who cannot hold a bow. If I dare to close my eyes, I have a terrible dream that comes to me night after night. Flying Heads come out of the forest, snarling and screaming, dripping blood. I think at first they are the spirits of my victims, but they are all the same face I see when I look into the still water of the lake. And when I wake, I cower in the dark, because the light itself has turned against me, blinding me, then pounding my head with some sorcerer's club."

Dekanawida asked, "Have you called in the medicine men?"

"I have had the best medicine men from all the villages," Atotarho said, "but they tell me the sorcery is too strong. I even had old Osinoh killed because I thought he was the cause, but nothing changed."

Dekanawida thought for a moment before responding, "Hiawatha was once thought to be the greatest of all living medicine men, known even among the Mohawks. Perhaps he could heal you."

And so it happened. The next day Hiawatha showed Atotarho how to make a tea of the herbs that Hiawatha had gathered at the lake. The tea lessened the pain of Atotarho's headaches. But Hiawatha told him that the headaches would keep coming back and the arm would die until he guessed the meaning of his dream. Hiawatha said that the illness was not caused by a sorcerer but by something within Atotarho's own spirit.

After several days, Atotarho realized what was wrong. He wept and said, "I am sick of war. I have no memories of joy, only of revenge and hatred. I have no friends, only slaves. When I am old I will be welcome at no hearth."

Hollow stump for grinding corn or herbs for medicine

Just as Hiawatha had predicted, Atotarho's headaches, paralysis, and terrible dreams all went away. The three men began to talk about the peace plan. Dekanawida told Atotarho that if he joined the alliance, the Onondagas would be the Fire Keepers and he would be the Head Principal Sachem. The council would always be held at the main Onondaga village.

Atotarho said, "That would be a good thing, since the Onondagas are in the center, with Oneidas and Mohawks to the east and Cayugas and Senecas to the west. How many sachems would we have at the council fire? The Mohawks will have nine. If the Oneidas also have nine, shouldn't the Onondagas have twice as many?"

Dekanawida told him that the Cayugas had already said they would not join unless they had ten representatives. "There are to be only fifty in all, so the Senecas would be left with only four, but they must have eight."

"Fourteen then," Atotarho said. "No fewer than fourteen. If the Onondagas are to join with the other nations, all our clans must be represented. If not, there will only be more trouble among the Onondagas. Besides that, if the Onondagas are always to host the council, we will have greater responsibilities. We will have to call the meeting and see to it that everything is done in accordance with the new law."

Hiawatha and Dekanawida agreed, although they worried that they might have difficulty with the Senecas, who would end up with fewer representatives than anyone.

Atotarho was not sure about paying for a life with wampum. It didn't seem like justice to him. He couldn't understand how it would work, but Hiawatha and Dekanawida explained how it was the most basic part of the whole plan.

Atotarho finally agreed to support the idea. "It might work," he said. "It could, I suppose."

By the time Atotarho called a council of the Onondaga sachems, rumors of his meeting with Hiawatha and Dekanawida had already spread from village to village. Some said that Hiawatha had become a sorcerer. Others said Atotarho's change of heart was Dekanawida's doing.

"Hiawatha's companion is a miracle worker," they declared. "He cannot speak clearly, but with his eyes, he can make the dead rise. He must indeed have a great power if he is able to change a snarling bear into a rabbit."

Still the people came from all over the Onondaga nation to see for themselves. And they found Atotarho changed! His usually tangled hair was combed and his customary sneer gone.

Relatives who had been separated gathered together in the longhouses. It was almost like a festival in the village.

Atotarho welcomed the sachems to the council fire. "For as long as any of us can remember we have been constantly at war," he told them. "Our children cannot roam in the woods. The women do not sleep at night. Laughter has been forgotten. It is the same with all Iroquois people. Tonight, as we sit here in the warmth of the council fire, the Cayugas plan revenge for our last raid. Their women weep over lost children.

"It is time to recognize that we people of the longhouse are all one family," he continued. "Dekanawida and Hiawatha have brought us a plan by which we can live in peace instead of war. The Mohawks have agreed to join with us; the Oneidas are ready to agree; the Cayugas would already be under the Tree of Peace except for fear of the mighty Onondaga nation. Only the Senecas have yet to be approached."

The sachems listened to Atotarho in disbelief. Then Dekanawida told of his vision of the eagle perched atop the Tree of Peace, and Hiawatha explained the three double principles and how they would be carried out. He told how they could use wampum belts to pass on the laws to their children and to other nations. These belts were like scrolls, with laws and history written on them.

After the sachems had heard everything—the vision, the plan, and Atotarho's renunciation of war—they passed a white calumet around the fire. A new day had come!

11

Peace

As Hiawatha and Dekanawida walked out through the gate of the Onondaga village, Atotarho met them and handed them a pouch.

"Here," Atotarho said, "take this to the Cayuga sachems so they will know that Atotarho wishes them to be his brothers. Let the shells say that I am tired of war and forever pledge myself to keeping the fire of peace."

Walking westward, the two friends were full of hope. No sooner had they entered the hunting grounds of the Cayugas than scouts spotted them. As Hiawatha and Dekanawida emerged from the river at the spot where countless war parties had crossed, three elders of the tribe—two sachems and a medicine man—greeted them. At the water's edge,

Dekanawida presented the elders with thirteen strings of wampum, in condolence for all Cayugas killed in war. Hiawatha offered his own strings of white wampum. Then he extended the white wampum Atotarho had sent, saying the very words that Atotarho said.

Although the Cayugas welcomed the men and their gifts, they had trouble believing that the Onondagas had actually joined the league. Furthermore, they were not happy to hear that the Onondagas would have fourteen representatives at the council fires.

"It is just as we feared," one of the sachems said. "We Cayugas will be outnumbered in peaceful matters just as we have been in war."

Hiawatha answered, "The Onondagas need more representatives because they have extra duties to perform. Since the council fire will always be held at the main Onondaga village, the Onondagas must make all the preparations. They must notify the other nations and make arrangements to accommodate all the guests. They will have to prepare the council fire and offer special prayers. They will have their hands full. But remember, they will have no more votes than the Cayugas."

The elders listened carefully and seemed satisfied with Hiawatha's explanation. But after a while, another sachem said, "It seems that other nations have special duties. What are the special duties of the Cayugas?"

Hiawatha answered, "Every matter that comes before the council will be considered on both sides of the fire."

One of the sachems asked, "What does this mean to be considered on both sides of the fire?"

Hiawatha said, "On one side of the fire will sit the Mohawks and Senecas, keepers of the two doors of the great longhouse of nations. Together, they will decide whether the matter should be considered by the council. Then, if the matter is accepted for consideration, all the Mohawk and Seneca sachems will discuss it until they come to an agreement. After the Mohawks and Senecas have agreed, the Cayugas and Oneidas, their younger brothers, will consider the matter until they too have agreed with each other. If both sides of the fire agree, the matter will be turned over to the principal Fire Keeper, Atotarho, who will sanction it."

"What if we can't agree?" asked the sachem. "What if one side of the fire decides in favor of a proposal and the other side decides against it?"

"Then the Fire Keeper will have to talk with his sachems and agree on which of the two alternatives is better. Everyone will have to abide by that decision," Hiawatha answered.

Hiawatha could still sense the reluctance of the Cayugas. He could understand their feelings very well. "I know it is hard for you to trust Atotarho, your old enemy," he told them. "But you must know that I myself have suffered greatly at his hands. I lost everyone who was dear to me. In fact, I once thought that I would never be free of my hatred for him. My bitterness and sorrow turned the world to ashes. The sorrow will always stay with me, but my hatred is gone. The old Atotarho has been destroyed."

The Cayugas trusted Hiawatha, and they had heard miraculous stories of Dekanawida. Perhaps it was true that the Creator had sent Dekanawida to bring peace among nations; perhaps he could even eliminate the evil that had twisted Atotarho. At last the elders agreed to take the plan before the rest of the Cayugas. "When you return from the land of the Senecas, we will give you our answer," they promised the two peacemakers.

The Cayugas brought their guests into the village to the medicine man's lodge, where they stayed for the night. The next morning, loaded down with provisions the Cayuga women insisted they take, the two men headed west with their message of peace.

As usual Hiawatha and Dekanawida stopped well outside the first Seneca village to build their fire and shelter so that the Senecas would know their intentions were peaceful. Again the two missionaries sent white wampum to the principal sachem and presented their cause.

Corn husk maskette

Midwinter Festival mask

Corn husk mask

The principal sachem of the Seneca village was a very old man whose hearing was not very good. With him were two younger sachems. The Senecas had heard rumors of an Iroquois alliance, and for a time they feared the other four nations might be conspiring against them. They were very wary.

The old sachem said, "We, too, have had enough of killing, but this alliance wouldn't help us. We are not afraid of Atotarho, nor do we need his protection. Seneca warriors are strong."

Hiawatha snapped a twig in two to show how easily a single arrow could be broken. "But," he said, "five arrows bound together with sinew have the strength of an oak branch."

The Senecas were silent, wondering if Hiawatha was threatening them when he said the Iroquois was greater than the lone Seneca nation, however strong.

"We have more trouble with crooked tongues to the north," the sachem said, "than with our Iroquois brothers. What good would this alliance be with them?"

Hiawatha said, "More than you think. Outsiders would not want to attack you if they knew they were going to have to deal with the whole league. They would let you live in peace. Besides, when the league becomes strong it will include all people, not just the five Iroquois nations."

The Senecas listened, but Hiawatha couldn't tell what they were thinking. He continued, "Every tribe in the league will have a special duty. The Senecas will be the Keepers of the Western Door, just as the Mohawks are the Keepers of the Eastern Door."

"Ha!" said the old sachem. "Then it is not you who will protect us, but we who will protect you!"

Hiawatha said, "Not at all. The special duty of the Keepers of the Western Door is to catch any dangerous crawling things that creep across the threshold. It would be your responsibility to keep the council from considering anything that might hurt the league."

The Senecas thought about this and seemed pleased. They talked long into the night, going over each point of the Iroquois laws. The old sachem looked closely at Hiawatha each time the peacemaker spoke, looking for a sign that Hiawatha was lying.

Finally the old man said, "It is a good thing. The laws are just. When the time is right, I shall speak with my people about the Great Peace."

On the way back, Hiawatha and Dekanawida stopped with the Cayugas, where they were welcomed as friends. True to their word, the Cayugas had held a council meeting. They would join the league.

As they traveled east, the two missionaries of the Great Peace were welcomed at each village. They were never hungry and never afraid. By the time they reached the Oneidas on their return journey, a year had passed. The Oneidas had decided to join the league.

A young Oneida sachem said, "At the council fire we heard how Hiawatha combed the snakes out of Atotarho's hair and Dekanawida smoothed the seven crooks out of his body. They say that he is now as handsome and wise as Dekanawida himself."

When the two friends reached the land of the Mohawks, a band of young boys met them deep in the forest. "Now we have the strongest nation on Earth!" one of the youths boasted. "Everyone everywhere will fear the mighty league of Iroqouis."

Dekanawida and Hiawatha tried to explain that the purpose of the league was to maintain peace, not to promote war; but the youths were so full of themselves that they paid little attention to what their heroes were saying.

Two of the boys were talking to each other about the change that had come over Atotarho. One of them said, "Dekanawida was watching Atotarho from the trees. He saw him going back and forth to the riverbank, taking water into his lodge."

"What was he doing with the water?" the other one asked.

"That's what Dekanawida wondered. Then he saw Atotarho drag this big, heavy basket into his lodge, so he climbed up on Atotarho's roof and looked down through the roof hole."

"So what was it?"

"Atotarho was getting ready to cook a human being."

"Come on!"

"No. It's the truth. My grandfather told me."

"So what did Dekanawida do? Did he try to stop him?"

"He didn't have to. Atotarho was looking into his pot, and he saw Dekanawida's reflection. But he didn't know it was Dekanawida's reflection; he thought it was his own. He said to himself, 'I didn't know I was so handsome. I'm too handsome to do such ugly things.'"

"Then what?"

"That was it. He decided he had to be a better person, and he dragged the pot out of the house and dumped it. After that he met Dekanawida and told him he would force the Onondagas to join the league."

Another boy who had been listening said, "You got the story all wrong. It wasn't Atotarho at all. That's how Dekanawida met Hiawatha."

Hiawatha smiled and said to Dekanawida, "This story shows the truth of one thing."

Dekanawida said, "Yes. It shows that we need to weave the laws of our league into wampum as soon as possible to keep them from changing before the first council fire."

12

Sunset

Not long after that the first Council of the Great Peace met. No one knows exactly when it took place, but some historians believe it was in 1570. Others, however, including many Iroquois, think the first council fire was built in the 1400s. Whenever it happened, the great work of Dekanawida and Hiawatha was largely done. What they called the Great Peace brought about the first republic on the American continent—the Iroquois League or Iroquois Confederacy, sometimes known as the Five Nations.

The new laws that made the Great Peace possible became the constitution of the Iroquois, although it was not written down until several centuries later. During all that time, the entire constitution was kept alive in the memories of men. Each of several men memorized a part of it and passed that part down to the next generation. However, without the symbols and counters of the wampum belts to aid their memories, those men might soon have forgotten the rules that bound their republic together.

According to legend, after he and Hiawatha had finished their work, Dekanawida stood on the shore of the lake from which he had first appeared and told his Mohawk friends that he would never again be seen on Earth. Then he climbed into a white canoe and paddled out from shore, growing smaller and smaller until he disappeared altogether. Some say he went to the Forest Beyond the Red Lakes of the Sunset. Others say he returned, to live with his mother's people in the land of the Hurons.

Hiawatha grew old among the Mohawks, where he was a respected sachem. He was always concerned with the practical side of government. According to some, he spent his later years clearing some of the trails between villages, making it easier for members of the various tribes to travel back and forth. By the time white people began to settle in what is now New York State, all the Iroquois villages were connected by a network of trails.

Many things have happened to the league in the more than 400 years since it was founded, but some things have not changed. Eventually, a sixth nation, the Tuscaroras, joined the league. Today the Iroquois League is split roughly in half, with one part on the Six Nations Reserve near Brantford, Ontario, in Canada, and the other still centered around Onondaga, New York. Together both groups still have fifty sachems, representing the original five tribes. Both have a Fire Keeper called Atotarho. The Canadian sachem is considered "acting" Atotarho. Of the fifty sachemships, whether north or south of the Canadian border, two have never been filled. Those two still belong to Hiawatha and Dekanawida.

Part Two:
The Legacy of
Hiawatha

13
New World

When that first Council of the Great Peace was held, sometime around 1570, the Iroquois League extended from Lake Ontario to the Susquehanna headwaters and from the mountains west of the Hudson River almost to Lake Erie, in what is now central and western New York. By 1750, when the league was at its strongest, it had expanded to include nearly 300,000 square miles, from the St. Lawrence River in the North almost to the Savannah River in the South; from the Hudson in the East to the Mississippi in the West. In other words, a quarter of a century before the American Revolution, the Iroquois controlled most of the land and most of the strategic waterways between what is now the Canadian city of Quebec to the northern border of Georgia, from the Appalachian Mountains to the Ohio and Mississippi rivers.

The world Hiawatha had dreamed of encompassed a great family of human beings living together in the peace of the longhouse. In fact, the League of Peace had been extended to include many nations. However, the old war parties also had grown. For every warrior who lived in Hiawatha's time, there were now a hundred. Although the Great Peace had quieted the small, ganglike wars, it contributed to far more devastating wars later.

For one thing, not everyone who had joined the Iroquois Confederacy was interested in peace. Some were more interested in trade advantages. Even before the Five Nations was established, various tribes had begun to trade essential goods. Certain tribes controlled the very hard stone, flint, that was necessary to make tools and weapons. Others supplied most of the tobacco used in ceremonies. Some had very valuable hunting lands, teeming with beaver and marten for furs. Still others made good nets and bows. Some modern writers insist that the Iroquois eventually became strong, not for peace, but to expand their fur trade.

Even so, for 150 years, only a few tribes joined the league willingly. Hiawatha, Dekanawida, and their missionaries had tried to persuade their close Iroquois neighbors to join them and come onto the Snow White Carpet of peace that was in Dekanawida's dream. But those nations refused.

Even after the establishment of the league, the Iroquois had not done particularly well against their enemies, often losing more scalps than they took. The Hurons were especially troublesome to the Five Nations. They were not interested in becoming a part of Dekanawida's vision and sent ever larger war parties into the league territory. The Mohawks and Senecas were constantly fighting the Hurons and Algonquins in small battles outside the villages and in hunting territories.

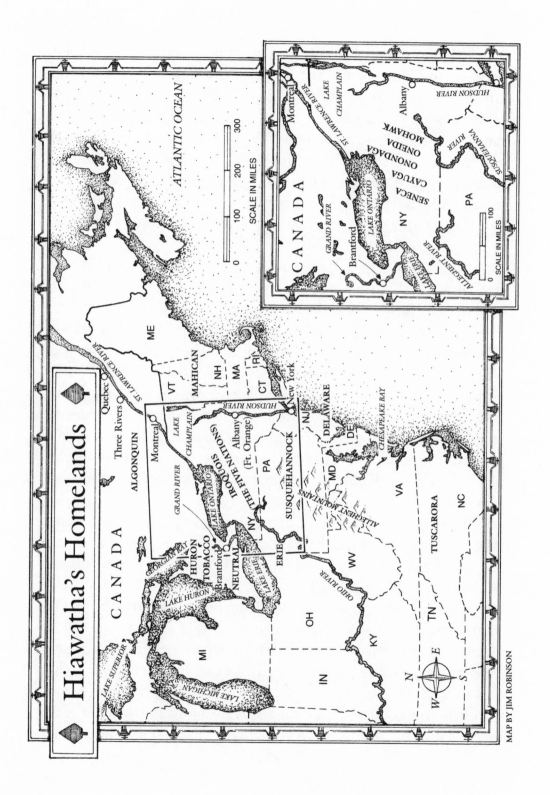

Hiawatha's Homelands

MAP BY JIM ROBINSON

The more peaceful Petuns and the Neutrals, who lived between the Hurons and the Senecas, did not wish to join the Great Peace either. They hadn't had the troubles with their other neighbors that the Five Nations had. For the most part, they minded their own business. The Petuns raised tobacco and bartered it with the Neutrals for flint. Only men were allowed to raise tobacco and mine flint, and perhaps this was why these tribes had less time for warfare. Or, possibly, their warlike neighbors didn't want to endanger their own supplies of these important goods.

The coming of white people also played a part in the terrible wars that occurred among the league and other tribes in the area. Jacques Cartier was the first white man to go up the St. Lawrence River. This was in 1535. Hiawatha might have heard rumors of Cartier's coming. The explorer met the Hurons, and old Huron men probably talked about the meeting as they sat around the hearth. But Cartier was around them for such a short time that he quickly became just another legend, part of the general mystery of the misty river and the "salt lake" beyond it. Just as Hiawatha could not have imagined the world of Cartier, Cartier did not understand the stone-age world he had entered.

The sight of such a huge sailing vessel and these light-skinned men with their strange clothing, tools, and guns was as remarkable to the Hurons as the landing of a ship full of Martians would be to earthlings today. The story of that first contact with white men spread from one village to the next, then from one tribe to the next, until it was woven into other legends of the past. Although there is no record of Cartier meeting the Iroquois, more than 150 years later Iroquois sachems told the Dutch of an amazing "winged" ship that had come into Iroquois country. They told of wanting to know what was in its belly. According to the sachems, their forefathers had made an agreement with a white man whose name was Jacques.

On his first voyage, Cartier mistook *canada,* the Huron word for "village," for the name of a kingdom. On his second trip, he thought he was in Mexico, visiting the kingdom of Canada, and he expected to find gold and precious stones to carry back to his king. To the Hurons and Algonquins, the most precious stones might well have been flint and *chert*, a hard rock used to make tools. They knew nothing of gold. Nevertheless, they led Cartier to an area they believed had precious stones. The confused explorer returned to France with worthless rocks. He also captured twelve Huron sachems and carried them back to Europe to verify his story of exploring Mexico. For some reason, Cartier had not realized the importance of the furs, which were as valuable as jewels in Europe at that time.

As soon as the French found out that Cartier had not been in Mexico after all and had not brought back gold and jewels, they lost interest in the land he had explored. Cartier never returned. But nearly 100 years later, another explorer, named Samuel de Champlain, arrived in the New World from France. The coming of Champlain eventually led to the end of the Iroquois way of life.

Champlain was a much better explorer than Cartier. He carefully mapped much of the Iroquois and Algonquin territory, then claimed it for France. On his second trip he started a permanent settlement, Quebec, which became the center of "New France" and the fur trade. During his early explorations, he made friends with many Algonquin tribes and with the Hurons, trading iron tools for their plentiful furs. These tools the Indians received changed their lives completely. As trading between the French and the Indians increased, the different tribes were no longer dependent on the Neutrals for a steady supply of flint for tool making. But they were now dependent on the French.

Old Broken-nose mask   Curing rite mask

The Hunchback mask

A few years after the fur trade began, the Iroquois lost many of their old tool-making skills. They no longer trained their sons and daughters as they had been trained. As metal pots replaced clay ones, there was no need for potters. As metal hoes replaced stone hoes and iron weapons replaced flint weapons, men and women did not sit beside the hearth making their own tools. Cheap European blankets replaced the furs that had kept Iroquois people warm through all the winters of their lives. In time wampum was no longer hand-cut from shells but was replaced by porcelain beads and machine-cut shells manufactured in Europe. Now the Europeans could trade a handful of cheap beads for very valuable furs.

The Hurons recognized the trading advantage they had over their old enemies, the Five Nations. Their thirty villages stood squarely between the French traders and the Iroquois League. To keep the French from doing business with the Five Nations, the Hurons told Champlain it was dangerous to travel in Iroquois territory. The traders told stories of Mohawk brutality, some true, some exaggerated. "Furthermore," the Hurons said, "these demons keep us from providing you with all the furs you need."

In 1609 the Hurons talked Champlain and a handful of Frenchmen into helping them attack a Mohawk war party. They approached the Mohawks by canoe, traveling along the shore of what is now called Lake Champlain. The Hurons told Champlain that his men should aim their guns at the sachems. Champlain later wrote, "When I saw them prepare to shoot their arrows, I raised my arquebus [an early type of portable gun] and, aiming directly at one of the chiefs, fired. Two of them fell dead at this shot and one of their companions received a wound from which he later died. I had put four balls in my arquebus." Champlain and the other Frenchmen chased the Mohawks into the woods, thinking they had frightened them into submission.

Instead of intimidating the Mohawks, this skirmish led to the Five Nations' lasting distrust and hatred of the French. Because of that distrust, the Five Nations refused to accept the French missionaries. That refusal led to an even larger break between the Hurons and the league, because the Hurons gradually became Christian, while the Five Nations continued to believe in their old gods.

Several years later, Champlain joined the Hurons in one more battle with the Five Nations. This time 200 armed men attacked an Iroquois village on Lake Onondaga. In spite of enemy guns, the Iroquois won, wounding Champlain himself. Their victory gave the Iroquois confidence in the face of white people's weapons.

Before long, more light-skinned people arrived. This time it was the Dutch, who settled even closer to the Iroquois lands. In 1623 the Dutch established Fort Orange (which the British later renamed Albany), just east of Iroquois hunting grounds. The Dutch were as interested as the French in trading furs—so interested that they eventually traded guns with the Indians for pelts. The Dutch didn't care whether the balance of power between the tribes was upset by the Indians having guns. They simply wanted to win the fur-trade war with the French. And they could keep the French from extending their fur trade any farther south by giving guns to the Indians.

In 1624 the league worked out a trade treaty with New France, only to have the Dutch turn the confederacy of Algonquins, called the Mahicans, against them, preventing the Iroquois from delivering their furs to the French. To make peace with the Mahicans, the Iroquois had to sign a secret trade agreement with the Dutch, negating the treaty they had just made with the French.

The longhouse people, whose idea of wealth was a year's supply of corn, were never a match for the greedy Europeans. The Iroquois were taught, as Hiawatha had been, that it was wrong to take more than one's share. Many of the Europeans, on the other hand, had come to the New World to make their fortunes. The richer they became, the better. When the Dutch had exhausted the supply of beaver pelts in the land of the Five Nations, they encouraged the Iroquois to invade the Algonquin hunting grounds that lay to the north. As a result, many warriors on both sides died.

In 1645 the French invited representatives of the Iroquois, Hurons, and Algonquins to meet with them at Three Rivers, south of Quebec. The French hoped to put an end to the terrible fighting and reach a trade agreement with all the tribes involved. To show the Iroquois their good intentions, the French returned those Iroquois who had been captured by the Hurons. In return, the league sent the sachem Kiotsaeton to represent

COURTESY MUSEUM OF THE AMERICAN INDIAN, HEYE FOUNDATION

*Reenactment of Hiawatha's legend given by the Iroquois
of the Cattaraugus Reservation, New York, in 1906*

them. Kiotsaeton returned Guillaume Couture, a Frenchman the league had held as a prisoner for three years.

With Couture acting as interpreter, Kiotsaeton stood offshore in the bow of his boat and presented the French with many strings of porcelain wampum. Each string was accompanied by a speech. It was the first recorded instance of the Iroquois using Dekanawida's River's Edge ceremony with white people to remember all those who had died in battle.

Kiotsaeton said, "I am the mouth for my whole country. You listen to all Iroquois when you hear my words. There is no evil in my heart. I have only good songs in my mouth." He then sang a song for the French governor, the naval commander, the Jesuit priest, and the sachems who were gathered for the meeting.

As he held up each string of wampum, he spoke on a different topic. The first string was to thank the governor for sparing the life of an Iroquois who had been captured the year before. The second reminded the governor that Kiotsaeton had just returned a French hostage. The third thanked the governor for the gifts he had sent the previous year with the returned prisoner. "Your gifts made the war clubs fall out of our hands," Kiotsaeton told the governor. The fourth string spoke of forgiveness of the Algonquins for the deaths they had caused among the Iroquois. He said that when his forefathers had seen that his heart was capable of revenge they had called out to him, reminding him of Hiawatha's message of forgiveness. As the afternoon passed, Kiotsaeton recited string after string. All invited peace among the nations gathered there.

But what Kiotsaeton really wanted was peace with the Hurons so that the Iroquois could set up trade with the French. He did not want peace with the Algonquins, because in spite of his "good songs," he and his people had not forgiven them for recent wrongs. However, the French governor didn't really want the Hurons and Iroquois to make peace with each other. Peace would mean the Hurons could sell their furs to the Dutch as well as to the French. Furthermore, the Algonquins really didn't want peace with the Iroquois, and neither did the Hurons. In the end, although the Three Rivers Treaty was signed, no lasting peace came from it. Within a year they were all back at war, and the Mohawks had killed a Jesuit priest who was attempting to set up a mission among them.

14

Great Peace by Conquest

For some time, the league had encouraged the Hurons to join as the sixth nation. But the Hurons hoped to divide the alliance, by negotiating with the separate nations. In 1648 they persuaded the Onondagas to enter into a trade agreement with the Susquehannocks and themselves. The Hurons also were working on a treaty with the Cayuga nation. Finally, however, the Hurons enraged the Mohawks and Senecas and brought about their own defeat.

That winter the Hurons were recovering from a terrible epidemic of smallpox that had killed nearly half their people. Although it had been a bitter winter, the people found comfort in their new religion—Christianity. Priests visited the villages regularly, teaching the Hurons to accept the suffering they had been through.

Only a few years before, the Dutch had sold the Iroquois 400 guns with which to defend the Dutch trading post. Armed with these guns, the Iroquois struck the Hurons while they were still weak from the epidemic. The snow was still deep and the lakes were frozen on March 16, 1649, when the Mohawks and Senecas swarmed into a Huron village. The raiders screamed bloodcurdling war cries. Some held firebrands, or pieces of burning wood, to the palisades; others streamed through the village gates, firing guns or swinging war clubs. Most of the people in the village were killed and scalped, but a few escaped through the deep snow to the Jesuit mission ten miles away. Leaving a handful of men to guard the village, the Iroquois army moved on to another Huron village.

At sunrise the next morning, the Mohawks and Senecas came screaming out of the forest, swinging their clubs. They met more resistance in the second village but quickly overcame the Hurons, killing and scalping everyone in sight. Within one week, they had sent the whole Huron nation running into the forest. Many Hurons collapsed in the snow and froze to death as they tried to reach the safety of the Jesuit mission or find refuge with other tribes. Those who were captured were adopted by the Mohawks and Senecas, and their land became hunting grounds for the league.

This terrible massacre fulfilled the prophecy that Dekana-wida, a Huron by birth, would be responsible for the destruction of his own people. The Iroquois went after the Hurons to stop them from dividing the league. However, there is no clear reason that explains why the Iroquois continued their war. One powerful war chief, another Atotarho, may have started it. Perhaps the Iroquois thought they were fulfilling their destiny and extending the White Carpet of Peace by bringing these people into the league. Perhaps they were controlled by the white people. Whatever the causes, once started on the warpath, the Iroquois continued to destroy their enemies, one by one.

In December 1649 the Iroquois League struck another Iroquois-speaking tribe, the Petuns, whose land was just south of the Huron nation. The Petuns were called the "Tobacco People" because they supplied other tribes with the tobacco smoked in peace pipes. Before they were wiped out by the Iroquois, the Hurons had both protected and dominated the Tobacco People. When the white people came, the Hurons acted as middlemen, first trading with the Petuns for the tobacco, then selling it at a profit to the French. After the Hurons were defeated, the Tobacco People dealt directly with the French but not with the Dutch. So the Dutch encouraged the Five Nations to take over the Petuns and their hunting lands.

The league attacked during a blinding snowstorm, burning and killing. It took the Iroquois warriors less than a week to overcome the 8,000 Tobacco People. The Petuns were not completely wiped out, as the Hurons had been, but they were forced to abandon their burned-out villages to the league. Enough of them escaped, however, to retain their tribal identity. They found refuge with the Ottawas.

In 1651 the league swooped down on the Neutrals, a tribe of ten thousand Iroquois who lived just south of the Petuns. The Neutrals were simple people, who had managed to stay out of trouble by using diplomacy with their more aggressive neighbors. The Neutrals are said to have made the league angry by harboring Hurons who had escaped the Iroquois invasion two years before. Eight hundred Senecas and Mohawks stormed into the land of the Neutrals, burning and looting their villages and scattering their people. Some Neutrals fled west, some south. One small group of survivors formed a small tribe.

Seventy-four years later, it was adopted by the league as the "seventh nation."

After attacking the Neutrals, the league did not go to war again for more than three years. But they looked at the lands of the Erie Indians with envy. The Eries controlled vast forests just south of the Neutrals and west of the Senecas. The Eries did not have firearms, but they used poison-tipped arrows. The Iroquois League put together the largest army yet, made up of braves from all Five Nations. In the autumn of 1654 the army struck. Although the league warriors wore bark armor, the first shower of the Eries' poison arrows killed many of them. Then the league attacked the largest Erie town with firebrands, swarming across the stockades and massacring its inhabitants. Because the Erie territory was so large, it took a long time to round up all the survivors. Those Eries who were found were then adopted by the league as full-fledged members and welcomed onto the White Carpet of Peace.

The next people the league destroyed were the Fire Nation, a group of Algonquins who roamed throughout the Michigan peninsula and the Midwest. These people didn't live in villages, so the league didn't attack them. Instead the league gradually ran the Fire Nation people off their customary hunting land, then used the territory for its own.

The last Iroquois war was in 1675 with the Susquehannocks, who lived just south of the Eries, along the Susquehanna River in Pennsylvania and Maryland. Their chief town was at the head of Chesapeake Bay. The Susquehannocks had fought often with the Senecas and Mohawks. They also had joined with the Hurons in an attempt to coax the Onondagas away from the league. Later the Europeans had given the Susquehannocks muskets with which to stop the league. However, the Senecas, Mohawks, and Cayugas attacked the Susquehannocks in 1675, completely destroying the nation, burning its villages, and killing hundreds of its people. Those who survived were adopted by the Senecas.

It had taken the Iroquois about twenty-five years to overrun most of their neighbors. As terrible as these wars were, the Iroquois did not oppress the people they had conquered. Once the battle was over, the Iroquois usually took their enemies into their own tribes and treated them exactly as they did their own citizens, just as they had adopted the prisoners taken in former times.

While the Iroquois were building their vast empire, the Algonquins were gradually being destroyed by the white people— by their muskets, their diseases, and their alcohol. The Dutch traders gave the Algonquins gin for fur; the English gave them rum and whiskey; the French traded brandy. White people visiting the villages reported seeing even very young children sick from alcohol abuse. The Jesuits had fought for many years to keep French fur traders from selling brandy to the Algonquins. They were not successful until a series of natural events convinced the government of New France that the Jesuits were right and brandy was wrong.

In 1662 either a comet or a series of meteors passed through the skies. According to Jesuit records, "A number of fires of various and quite eccentric shapes were seen flying through the air. Over Quebec and Montreal there appeared one night a globe of fire diffusing a great light." Some Montreal viewers thought the "globe of fire" had broken off the moon.

A few months later, the record continues, "three apparent suns were seen at once on a line parallel to the horizon." The next month Quebec experienced a great earthquake. "The whole surface of the earth assumed an appearance like that of a stormy sea. Whole mountains were uprooted and moved from their bases. Some were thrown amid rivers, blocking their courses." One nun had a vision of four demons shaking the city by its four corners.

Convinced that this was a warning from heaven, the French traders stopped selling brandy to the Algonquins for several years.

Even though the Algonquins feared the Iroquois, who were famous for sometimes burning and torturing their victims, they now feared the settlers even more—especially the Dutch and the English. The French accepted the Indian people as equals. The French trappers took Algonquin and Huron wives. The Jesuits risked their own lives to convert the native population. But the Dutch and English settlers didn't think of the native people as true human beings, but as part of the wilderness itself. Some of the English colonists hunted the native people like animals, offering bounties for the scalps of women and children.

The Delaware, a large and advanced Algonquin tribe, known to other coastal tribes as "the original human beings," had tried to do business with the white people, only to be taken advantage of. At one point, their sachem, Tamenend (called Tammany by the whites), had "sold" all the land between the Delaware and the Susquehanna rivers to William Penn for two guns, six blankets, twelve coats, and four kettles. Penn believed the sale was a valid one, even though he knew he was cheating the Indians. But the Delaware didn't understand the transaction. They had thought the sale meant that the white settlers would share the land with them, not take it from them. But the white people soon surveyed the land and marked it off into parcels, driving the Delaware away. In 1712 the Delaware, having no place to go, asked the Iroquois to take them into the league.

The league took "the original human beings" in, but limited their power. The league gave them land, but it made "women" out of them. That is, they had all the privileges of Iroquois citizenship, but they were not allowed to engage in war. The Delaware, however, did not accept their limited role for long and many moved farther west, across the Allegheny Mountains.

About the same time, the Tuscarora nation, an Iroquois tribe that had settled in the Carolinas, began moving north and asked to be taken into the league. The Tuscarora sachems were accepted as the sixth member of the governing council of sachems in the league. However, they were not represented at the council fire, since the fifty places were already filled. In 1722 the council officially changed the name of the league to "League of Six Nations."

The league took in thousands of Indians who fled from the white settlers. Many settled in the forests of Pennsylvania. After some of these ungrateful newcomers began selling Iroquois land to the white people, the Iroquois appointed a territorial governor—the Oneida sachem, known in English as John Shikellamy. The council notified the white people that if they purchased the Iroquois land from anyone besides Shikellamy, the sale would not be valid.

John Shikellamy was as good an administrator as anyone in America and won the full respect of the white people he dealt with. One of the first things he did as governor was to threaten the William Penn agents with war if they didn't stop selling liquor to the already battered people who had found refuge in Iroquois territory. The English settlers stopped the rum and whiskey sales.

15

Downfall

In 1664 the British took over from the Dutch the rule of what is now New York State. Almost from the start, the Iroquois got along well with the British. The British officials had a different style than the Dutch or the French. They dealt with the league as a sovereign nation. In 1710 the British invited five Mohawk sachems to London and treated them as if they were royal visitors. When the sachems first arrived, they wore fine buckskins, moccasins, colorful blankets, and silver and eagle feathers in their hair. Although the English people who had seen them were fascinated, their hosts thought the Mohawks should be dressed more suitably before being presented to Queen Anne. Theater dressers were hired to create costumes for the sachems. The costumers replaced the sachems' apparel with black breeches, frilly shirts, and silk stockings. They made the sachems scarlet capes trimmed in gold, and silver-buckled shoes, and replaced their feathers with cocked hats. The queen and the sachems both appreciated the finery.

The French must have envied the results of the trip. Only fifty years earlier, three of their Jesuit priests had been killed by the Mohawks, who had wanted no part of Christianity. Now this same tribe invited Queen Anne to send her Anglican missionaries to live among them, and when the sachems returned to America they immediately had a chapel built as the center of their new mission.

When the American Revolution broke out in 1776, the Six Nations wanted to remain neutral as trouble began to develop between the American colonists and the British. The Six Nations were not concerned with why the two sides were fighting, only with the ways they had been treated by the two groups. However, as the troubles between the Americans and the British grew worse, the Iroquois decided to join the British. The Iroquois felt that the British officials had treated them with dignity, while the American farmers had treated them with contempt. In addition, the Iroquois had more in common with the British than with the Americans. Most of the American farmers were rude, uneducated people. They had little power and were terrified of the wilderness in which they lived. Iroquois men were never farmers, and the wilderness was their beloved home. On the other hand, the British officials lived in great houses, represented powerful people, and were often adventurers. Furthermore, these powerful people made treaties and trade agreements with the Iroquois leaders.

Perhaps the most important single influence on British-Iroquois relations was Sir William Johnson, who first came to New York in 1740 from England. Sir William wanted two equally important things out of life—to have a good time and to build a large estate. He did both.

Johnson had a gift for fitting in with any group. He was equally at home with the Mohawks as he was with his fellow aristocratic British. The Mohawks even adopted him. As Warraghiyageh (his Mohawk name), Johnson learned to speak their language and sing their songs. Whenever he stayed in a Mohawk village, he dressed and painted himself like a Mohawk and participated in their rituals. He was good at their sports. The Mohawks liked him so much that they gave him huge land grants for himself and his children.

On this land, Sir William built two mansions—Johnson Hall and Johnson Castle. He filled them with liveried servants who called him "Your Lordship" and treated him like the baronet he was. Once a year he invited warriors from all the nations to Johnson Hall, where they held a three-day tournament of Iroquois games.

Johnson married Mary Brant, who was one-quarter white and three-quarters Mohawk. When Johnson died, two years before the American Revolution, he had an Episcopal service, a Masonic service, and an Iroquois service. All the sachems from the council of the Six Nations attended his funeral. Largely because of Johnson, the Mohawks, Senecas, Cayugas, and Onondagas remained loyal friends of the British in the war to come.

Johnson had taken a great interest in the education of his brother-in-law, Joseph Brant. He sent young Joseph to study at Eleazer Wheelock's Indian School and also took him along on several Mohawk war parties and raids. Not long before Johnson died, he sent the young man to England, where some say Joseph became more British than the British. In 1776, when the American Revolution came, Joseph was commissioned a colonel in the British Army. He was given the duty of recruiting Iroquois warriors to conduct war parties against the American settlements. He was both an excellent recruiter and leader.

Another Indian leader in the American Revolution earned less respect. Red Jacket, so-called because he always wore a red coat from the British Army, was a Seneca who was known to have run from danger. Joseph Brant disliked him and called him "Cow Killer," referring to a time that Red Jacket's men returned from battle to find him butchering a cow that had belonged to one of the warriors. Apparently, Red Jacket had not expected the warrior to survive the fight. Several times Red Jacket was accused of attempting to double-cross Brant and a great Seneca sachem, Corn Planter. Although Red Jacket was unreliable, at times he showed valor in battle and was later made a sachem by his tribe. He did not, however, have the strong ties to the British that Brant had, nor did he admire Brant's commitment. He thought Brant was a fool, who allowed the British to use him.

When the war ended, most of the Iroquois were forgotten by their British allies and were forced by the Americans to retreat into Canada. The once great League of Six Nations had been torn apart by the white man's war. The council itself had remained neutral and allowed the member nations to choose their own course; nevertheless, the American victory divided the league. The Oneidas and some Tuscaroras had fought on the side of the colonists, while the other four nations supported the British. The four nations had lost everything.

Joseph Brant fared better than the others who served the British. He received a six-mile-square land grant on the Grand River in Ontario and was retired at half pay. In his later years he became a scholar, translating the Gospel of Mark and the Book of Common Prayer into Iroquois. His mother's people made him a sachem.

In 1784 the part of the league that had moved north to Canada was granted a reserve on the Grand River as a reward for their service to the British. The Tuscaroras and Oneidas, who had remained loyal to the American colonists, were forced to give up most of their land to the state of New York. Illegal and questionable purchases and treaties deprived the Cayugas, Senecas, and Onondagas of their lands as well. The Americans sometimes appointed their own "chiefs" from among the tribes, then tricked them into signing away ancestral land. Just as most of the Iroquois had feared, the Americans would not deal with the league as a sovereign nation as had been the British custom.

16

Handsome Lake

E ven without the American Revolution, Hiawatha's world was doomed from the moment white Europeans entered it. This was not because white people were bad but because they were different. They had different beliefs, different ways of doing things, and even different ideas about what a family should be.

The tools the Europeans introduced quickly transformed the way the Iroquois people lived. As saws replaced axes, logs and boards replaced the bark coverings of the longhouses. Hinged doors replaced the hides that had hung over entrances. Fireplaces with chimneys replaced open hearths and roof holes.

More importantly, when plows were introduced to the Iroquois, their society changed completely.

According to the religious laws, only women were allowed to tend the food crops. But the women were not strong enough to pull the plows. Before men and animals could replace women in the cornfields, the Iroquois religious beliefs would have to change.

Money and the absolute ownership of land changed the Iroquois world even more than the new tools did. The Indians had traded much land and goods to the white people for cheap, machine-made wampum. After the American Revolution, however, the white people no longer accepted wampum as a form of money. Now the Iroquois had nothing to trade and no way to support themselves. Even if they had wanted to, they could not have returned to their old ways because they could no longer make their own tools. And, with less land, they couldn't trap enough furs to trade for the goods they needed. In this new world, they needed money, but they had few ways of getting it. One of the few ways they could get money was to sell off more of their land. They might have sold it all, had it not been for a new religious prophet named Handsome Lake.

Handsome Lake began his ministry in 1799. He was not a mystic, as Dekanawida had been. He was Corn Planter's ne'er-do-well half brother, and up to that point his life had been ruined by alcohol. Just as Hiawatha had grieved over the destruction of his people by the cycle of revenge, Handsome Lake now grieved over a different kind of destruction. Because of alcohol, families were no longer strong. Children went uncared for; men and women quarreled. Because of greed and lack of food, the Indians no longer shared what they had, and they were quickly selling off what was left of their land. Because they were ignorant of white people's ways, the Indians were easily cheated.

Handsome Lake never claimed to have supernatural powers. He was quick to admit that he was far from perfect. He was

irritable and did not get along well with people. But he claimed that his teachings were inspired by the Creator. Just as Dekanawida once had a vision, so also did Handsome Lake. In his vision, Handsome Lake had seen Indians turned into beasts because of alcohol. He preached that alcohol was only meant for white people. It was poison for the Iroquois people, and they must stop using it. Handsome Lake also had seen that the Creator did not intend land to be treated as merchandise. He told his people that they must keep the land and cultivate it for their children.

Handsome Lake taught the Iroquois that there were three things the white people did that the Iroquois also should do. He said, "First, the white man works on a piece of ground and harvests food for his family, so if he should die they still have the land for help." This idea was completely different from the old, longhouse way of doing things. The women owned the longhouse, cultivated the land, and harvested the food. Furthermore, owning land and passing it on to one's immediate family, as Handsome Lake was suggesting, was unknown among the Iroquois.

Handsome Lake said the second thing the Iroquois should copy from the white people was the way they built their houses. "He [the white man] builds it warm and fine appearing, so if he dies the family still has the house for help." In the past, when the villages moved every ten or fifteen years, the bark houses were not expected to last. The appearance of the house didn't matter. Most importantly, the family property passed from mother to daughter, not from man to wife or children.

"Finally," Handsome Lake said, "the white man keeps horses and cattle, so if he dies his family has the stock for help." In the old Iroquois world, there was no livestock, either for plowing or for food. Ownership of such animals would change the way the Iroquois worked and ate. Livestock would become a new kind of property to be passed on.

Handsome Lake called this new way of living the "New Religion." Along with the New Religion, it was Handsome Lake who introduced the plow to the Iroquois, the tool that changed their way of life forever.

At first only a few people followed Handsome Lake's teachings, but as the older people died, the New Religion caught on. Gradually, the Iroquois people began living as the white people did—farming, owning animals, and living in individual houses headed by men.

Handsome Lake also advised the Iroquois to become educated in the white people's language and ways, not to be *like* the white people but to do business with them. Most of what he taught was very practical and helped the Iroquois survive in the New World. But Handsome Lake also took care to preserve enough of Hiawatha's world to make his people feel at home. The longhouse has survived as a combination town hall and church, where Iroquois still conduct most of their tribal affairs. Although some present-day Iroquois are Christian, the ancient games have survived, and so have the festivals. The Iroquois New Year is still celebrated much as it was in Hiawatha's time, with dances, discussions of dreams, and the appearances of the Big Heads and False Faces.

Still there are those today who blame Handsome Lake for the loss of the old ways and who wish to return to the beliefs of Dekanawida and Hiawatha.

17
The Mystery

Many scholars believe the government set up by the Americans was based largely on the Iroquois government. There is no doubt that the United States government is similar to the confederacy established by Hiawatha and Dekanawida. The question is: Did the Iroquois have a direct influence on the colonists? Or was it just coincidence that the Americans came up with precisely the same form of government?

What are the similarities between the two governments? The first is the voluntary joining together of separate states or nations into one country, or federation. Next is a representative government, in which each state or nation sends a certain number of representatives to the central government to consider all problems that affect the whole federation. Just as the United States Constitution provides for each state to be equally represented in the Senate, the Iroquois Constitution provides one vote for each nation. Just as United States citizens have the privilege of choosing the representative they send to Washington, D.C., the women of the clans voted to select their representatives at the council fire. And just as United States citizens have the right to recall a representative, so did the people of the longhouses.

The United States government's system of "checks and balances" has kept any one person or branch of government from becoming too powerful. For example, the United States Constitution provides for "separation of powers" by setting up three branches of government—the executive, the legislative, and the judiciary. This system keeps one branch of government from making all the decisions.

The league also had a system of "checks and balances." For instance, the two sides of the council fire are like the two houses of Congress—the House of Representatives and the Senate. The Senecas and the Mohawks considered all proposals first, then passed them to the Cayugas and Oneidas, who then considered them. The Onondagas only voted in cases when the two sides of the fire disagreed; otherwise they simply validated whatever solution the other four tribes proposed. The role of the Onondagas was a little like the role of the vice president of the United States, who can break tie votes in the Senate, and the president, who signs into law what the two houses have agreed upon. However, unlike the United States president, the Iroquois Fire Keeper did not have the right to vote down (or veto) something the two sides had agreed upon.

Another similarity between the two governments was the importance of the constitution. The United States Constitution is "the supreme law of the land," above any leader or other

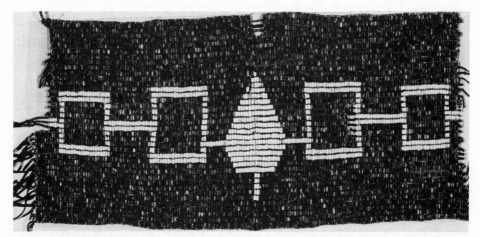

Iroquois wampum belt, symbolizing the League's formation. Four of the five founding nations are represented by rectangles. Onondaga, the central nation, is symbolized by the Tree of Peace. All five nations are linked by paths that extend out toward other nations.

laws. So was the Iroquois Constitution. Most Americans believe their Constitution was the first written constitution. That is, before that time no country had one single document that defined its government. However, the League of Six Nations had a written document. It was not written on paper, but it was woven in wampum beads and engraved in the minds of those men responsible for preserving it from one generation to the next. When the United States republic was born, the only similar government on Earth was that of the League of Six Nations.

One difference between the two governments is how the constitution's laws are interpreted. In the United States government the Supreme Court is responsible for this. For the Iroquois, this responsibility fell to the Keepers of the Doors—the Mohawks and Senecas—who decided what was worthy of discussion by the council.

The philosopher John Locke is credited with having had the greatest influence on those who wrote the United States Constitution. Locke, who was born in England in 1632, challenged the divine right of kings to rule. He believed the rights of ordinary people were more important than the arbitrary desires of a monarch, and that a leader who didn't serve the needs of the people had no right to rule and should be removed from office.

Locke believed citizens should have the right to worship as they please, to think as they please, and to say what they please. And, unlike the American founding fathers, Locke believed in equal rights for women. Just like the Iroquois, he thought that the only right human beings give up when they consent to be governed is the right to take justice into their own hands.

Locke died in 1704, years before the Declaration of Independence was signed. But there is no doubt that Locke's ideas influenced those who wrote the Constitution. Some parts of the declaration are almost word for word from Locke's *Second Treatise*. Many wonder, however, whether some of Locke's ideas came from reports that reached him from the New World on the Iroquois lifestyle. Did he know that the Iroquois people also had to give up the right to take justice into their own hands in order to make their government work?

No one really knows whether Locke's beliefs were influenced by the Iroquois. But the beliefs of Thomas Jefferson, Benjamin Franklin, and others certainly were. J.N.B. Hewitt, a Tuscarora, studied the American Indian cultures for the Smithsonian Institution. By the time he died in 1937, he was one of the foremost authorities on Iroquois life. He found written proof that the colonists knew of the Iroquois government.

In 1744 the colonial governors met in Lancaster, Pennsylvania, with the great Onondaga sachem Canassatego. The sachem quoted from the Iroquois Constitution, then advised the governors ". . . Our wise forefathers established Union and Amity among the Five Nations. This has made us formidable;

this has given us great weight and authority with our neighboring Nations. We are a powerful Confederacy; and by your observing the same methods, you will acquire such strength and power. Therefore, whatever befalls you, never fall out with one another."

Benjamin Franklin knew about the Iroquois government. Ten years after the Lancaster meeting, he attended a conference in Albany, near the heart of the Six Nations. That conference had been called to discuss the Albany Plan of Union, which would join together the colonies to form "one general government." Franklin declared there that if the many Iroquois tribes could establish a union and make it work for so long, then surely ten or a dozen English colonies could make a similar union work as well.

Hewitt also found that in 1775 there was a meeting between sachems from the League of Six Nations and delegates from the Continental Congress who were trying to keep the league neutral in the event of a war. Colonel Turbot Francis also had been at the Lancaster meeting with Canassatego thirty years earlier. He said that the colonists still remembered the advice Canassatego had given them, and they were following it. They were now bound together like the Iroquois nations, with "one head, one mind, one body, and one life."

The colonists used many ideas to develop their new government. They borrowed from Locke, from the English Bill of Rights, from the English Common Law, and from the laws of ancient Rome and Greece. It is possible that they were prouder of using the ideas of white philosophers and of great civilizations than they were of using the ideas of people they regarded as "savages." It is probable that the Iroquois Constitution gave them the ideas they needed to make it easier for them to survive in the civilized world.

18

Legacy of the Iroquois

Few people have recognized the influence of the Iroquois Constitution on the United States Constitution. But the Iroquois effect on Communism is well known.

In the mid-1800s, a Republican corporation lawyer named Lewis H. Morgan joined a men's social club called the Grand Order of the Iroquois. The purpose of the club was simply to have fun, and didn't have anything at all to do with the real Iroquois people. Morgan, however, became curious about actual Iroquois customs and began to visit a Seneca reservation that was not far from his own hometown of Rochester, New York. There he met Ely Parker, an engineer and brigadier general in the army. Parker was also the half-white grandson of Red Jacket. He and Morgan soon became good friends.

Before long, Morgan had learned enough about the League of the Iroquois to inspire him to find out more about these Indians. With Parker, Morgan visited many Seneca longhouses and learned firsthand about the Iroquois way of life. By 1851 he had gathered enough information on the history, structure, and customs of the league to publish a book called *The League of the Ho-De-No-Sau-Nee*. Morgan's book was one of the first to present careful observations of American Indians. The book suddenly made him the world's foremost specialist in ethnology, which is the study of culture. Parker's contributions to the book made it all the more believable.

In 1859, eight years after Morgan's first book came out, Charles Darwin published one of the most influential books ever written, *Origin of the Species*. In this book Darwin presented his ideas about evolution. He believed human beings and other life forms had developed their present characteristics

Laughing beggar mask

115

over a very long period of time. He thought that every species of living things had either adapted to their changing environment or died out—"survival of the fittest." He suggested that all life, including human beings, had the same origin.

Darwin was talking about physical changes, but many people applied his ideas to social conditions. Morgan was one of them. In 1877 he published a second book on the Iroquois, called *Ancient Society*. Morgan believed all people eventually go through the same social stages, from "savagery" to "barbarism" to "civilization." He believed all stages were presently represented on the planet. Furthermore, he was certain that he, Lewis H. Morgan, lived in an enlightened "civilized" state, one of the end products of nature's drive toward perfection. He believed the Iroquois society, which he had observed over the years, had not yet evolved into that state. The Iroquois were still in the "savage," or first, stage of social development. Consequently, as Morgan saw it, the Iroquois allowed civilized societies an opportunity to look at their own past, to see themselves as they had been before.

Morgan was a wealthy, powerful man who was more advantaged than the Iroquois people he visited. He could read and write. He traveled. He ate well. He lived in a comfortable house with servants. Although he had devoted many years to studying the Iroquois, he had probably not observed the way the poor people in his own society lived. It is probable that he believed the poor people in his "civilized" society were not as "fit" as those who were rich.

The Smithsonian Institution supported Morgan's work with grants, which helped spread his theories around the world. In London, two German philosophers, Karl Marx and Friedrich Engels, read Morgan's books with great interest. These two men thought the world had taken a wrong turn somewhere. They

believed capitalism hurt more people than it helped. They didn't think poor people were poor because they were less "fit" than rich people but because they didn't have any control over their own lives. Marx and Engels also believed all modern societies had one thing in common, no matter what type of government they had: Whoever owned the means of production had all the power.

Morgan's book *Ancient Society* provided them with a scientific explanation for what had gone wrong. Once the Iroquois had peacefully shared the harvest and the longhouse. Capitalism had come about when families began to live in separate houses and own separate flocks. From that time on, the men who owned the land, the livestock, and other property could force others to work for them; it was up to them to decide what the workers would receive for their efforts. In order for capitalism to work, the workers always had to receive less than their work was actually worth. Marx and Engels argued that a just society had to be closer to the Iroquois way of life than to capitalism.

Within a few years of reading *Ancient Society*, Engels published *Origin of the Family, Private Property and the State in Light of the Researches of Lewis H. Morgan*. This book, which was translated into English in 1902, quickly became one of the two basic texts of Communism, along with Marx's *Das Kapital*. Lenin, the first premier of the Soviet Union, tried to model the new Russian society after Engels' book. In fact, *Ancient Society* is sometimes referred to as the Old Testament of Communism.

Because of Morgan and the Russian interest in Iroquois life, the true story of Hiawatha may be better know in the Soviet Union than in America.

19

Recognition

Hiawatha wanted to change the world. According to the myths he lived by, that world was an island on a turtle's back, distant in every way from our own. According to today's historians, his group of warring tribes comprised only a few thousand people. How, then, did he reach through time and space to shape our twentieth-century world?

Hiawatha's and Dekanawida's ideas were so simple that they have not been officially recognized as ideas. Thomas Jefferson believed the American Indians "never submitted themselves to any laws, any coercive power, any shadow of government." In other words, he didn't recognize their Council of the Great Peace as a governing body, or their wampum constitution as law.

When Benjamin Franklin wrote the Albany Plan of Union in 1754, he took many ideas from the League of the Iroquois. Its Grand Council was to have elected members, representing ten colonies. These forty-eight members would meet once a year. Even though Franklin acknowledged that the Iroquois had successfully formed such a union, he still referred to them as "ignorant savages."

Not even Friedrich Engels recognized the basic idea of the Iroquois government. He thought the Iroquois just naturally lived together in harmony.

Until recently no one but the Iroquois people themselves have recognized the humble source of these ideas that changed

This newspaper cartoon by Benjamin Franklin appeared on May 9, 1754, just before the Albany conference between the Iroquois and the colonists. The drawing expressed Franklin's belief that the eleven colonies should unite under one central government. The Albany Plan of Union was based on the League of Iroquois' government.

the course of world history. White people in powdered wigs gave those concepts names such as "federation," "representative government," "referendum," and "constitution." They also took credit for the ideas themselves. But the truth is "We the people of the United States" owe a great deal to the ideas and eloquence of Hiawatha and Dekanawida, two "ignorant savages" who founded the first republic of its kind in the world.

Suggested Reading

Bierhorst, John. *The Naked Bear: Folktales of the Iroquois*. New York: Morrow, 1987.

Jones, Hettie. *Longhouse Winter: Iroquois Transformation Tales*. New York: Holt Rinehart and Winston, 1972.

Josephy, Alvin M., Jr. *The Patriot Chiefs*. New York: Viking Press, 1961.

Longfellow, Henry Wadsworth. *Song of Hiawatha*. New York: Platt & Munk Publishers, 1963.

ADVANCED READING:

Beauchamp, William. *The Iroquois Trail*. New York: AMS Press, 1976.

Fenton, William Nelson. *The False Faces of the Iroquois*. Norman, OK: University of Oklahoma Press, 1987.

Henry, Thomas. *Wilderness Messiah: The Story of Hiawatha and the Iroquois*. New York: Sloane Assoc., 1955.

SUGGESTED READING

Jennings, Francis. *The History and Culture of Iroquois Diplomacy.* Syracuse, NY: Syracuse University Press, 1985.

Mallery, Arlington. *The Rediscovery of Lost America.* New York: Dutton, 1979.

Wilson, Edmund. *Apologies to the Iroquois.* New York: Vintage Books, 1960.